SINGER® DESIGN

color
AND
design
ON
fabric

CREATIVE
PUBLISHING
international

MINNETONKA, MINNESOTA

President/CEO: David D. Murphy
Vice President/Editorial: Patricia K. Jacobsen
Vice President/Retail Sales & Marketing: Richard M. Miller

Color & Design on Fabric created by: The Editors of Creative Publishing
international, Inc., in cooperation with the Sewing Education
Department, Singer Sewing Company. Singer is a trademark of The
Singer Company Limited and is used under license.

Executive Editor: Elaine Perry
Project Managers: Linnéa Christensen, Amy Friebe
Senior Editor: Linda Neubauer
Senior Art Director: Stephanie Michaud
Project & Prop Stylist: Joanne Wawra
Sewing Staff: Arlene Dohrman, Sharon Ecklund, Joanne Wawra,
    Julann Windsperger
Technical Photo Stylists: Sharon Eklund, Bridget Haugh,
    Kathleen Smith
Studio Services Manager: Marcia Chambers
Photo Services Coordinator: Carol Osterhus
Photographers: Tate Carlson, Rebecca Schmitt, Joel Schnell
Publishing Production Manager: Kim Gerber
Desktop Publishing Specialist: Laurie Kristensen
Production Staff: Patrick Gibson, Michelle Peterson
Consultants: Diane Bartels, Robin Neidorf,
    Wendy Richardson, Julann Windsperger
Contributors: Decart, Inc.; Dharma Trading Company; Rupert,
    Gibbon & Spider, Inc.; Screen Trans Development Corporation;
    Silkpaint Corporation

Printed on American paper by:
    R. R. Donnelley & Sons Co.
    10 9 8 7 6 5 4 3 2 1

Creative Publishing international, Inc. offers a variety of how-to books. For
information write:
    Creative Publishing international, Inc.
        Subscriber Books
        5900 Green Oak Drive
        Minnetonka, MN 55343

Library of Congress Cataloging-in-Publication Data

Color and design on fabric.
        p. cm. -- (Singer design)
    Includes index.
    ISBN 086573-869-6 (hardcover) -- ISBN 0-86573-870-x (softcover)
    1. Dyes and dyeing, Domestic. 2. Textile painting. 3. Textile printing. 4. Appliqué. 5.
Color in textile crafts. I. Creative Publishing International. II. Singer design series.

TT853.C65 2000
746.6--dc21   99-054247

•••••••• Table of Contents ••••••••

Julann Windsperger

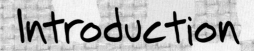

Introduction

When the fabrics you find aren't quite what you have in mind, consider their potential!

Flex your imagination and breathe fresh creativity into your sewing projects, whether they be quilts, home decor, garments, or gifts. Prepare to embark on a new journey of artistic discovery in a world where you determine and develop the color and design of the fabric. Learn how to apply fiber-reactive dyes and fabric paints to transform your ideas into visually captivating cloth, with schemes and patterns that reflect your own personality. Build depth and character, with user-friendly methods like screen printing, stenciling, or stamping. Use your new creations or found fabrics as backgrounds for expressive free-motion machine embroidery or fanciful appliqués. Stud the fabric surface with beadwork or add glimmering foil accents. Now you are at the helm from the very start. Jump on board and enjoy the ride!

... Playing with Color

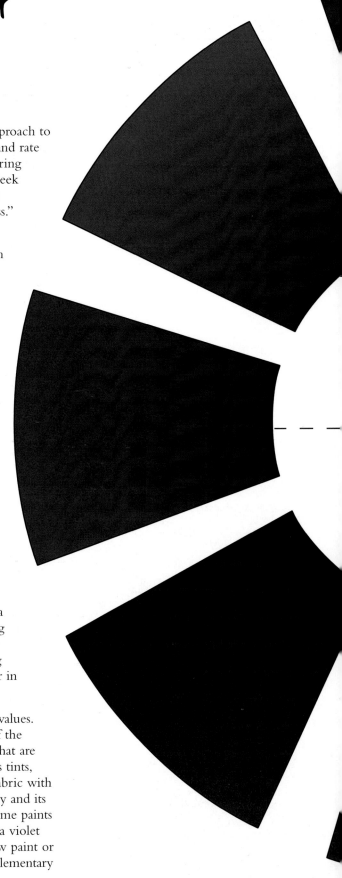

Unless you are already an expert on color, your least threatening approach to the subject is to learn as you go. Enjoy the experimenting process, and rate your attempts on a scale of "oops!" to "smashing success," remembering that even the most undesirable results have taught you something. Seek the reactions of others as well, because the interpretation of color is very personal; one artist's "oops!" may be another's "smashing success."

Increase your odds of achieving success with an understanding of basic color theory. Refer to the color wheel for a visual guide when planning a color scheme for your fabric. The *primary colors*—red, yellow, and blue—are the three foundation colors of the wheel. All other colors are combinations of these colors, and they are the only three colors that cannot be achieved by mixing others. The *secondary colors*—green, orange, and violet—are the colors you get when you mix two primary colors. *Tertiary colors* result when you mix a primary and a secondary color. *Complementary colors* are located directly across the color wheel from each other.

It is important to keep in mind that the color wheel explains color in a very simplified form, based on the colors of light. Mixing dye or paint colors is a bit more complicated, because some colors are stronger than others in *value:* their lightness or darkness. For instance, you will not get a true secondary green by mixing equal parts blue and yellow. Blue paint or dye has a darker value and is much more influential in the relationship, so the green color you want is best achieved by mixing blue into yellow, a small amount at a time.

Intensity refers to the strength or purity of the color. The pure colors form the outer ring of the color wheel. The intensity of a color is lessened by adding a small amount of its complementary color, thus creating a *tone. Shades* are achieved by mixing black into a color; blue plus black equals navy blue. *Tints* are achieved by mixing white into a color; red plus white equals pink. This makes sense for paint, but there is no such thing as white dye. White fabric showing through transparent dye creates the tint. The amount of dye powder in the dye bath determines the degree of the tint.

The most interesting color schemes include elements with various values. *Monochromatic color schemes* are made up of tints, shades, and tones of the same color, usually a sure success. *Analogous schemes* include colors that are adjacent to each other on the color wheel, and may include various tints, shades, or tones of each. A good rule of thumb when designing a fabric with a *complementary color scheme* is to use one of the colors predominantly and its complement as an accent color. Also, keep in mind that dyes and some paints are transparent. If you stamp a yellow transparent paint design over a violet background, the design will turn a muddy brown. An opaque yellow paint or flowing lines of yellow embroidery, however, will result in the complementary scheme you intended.

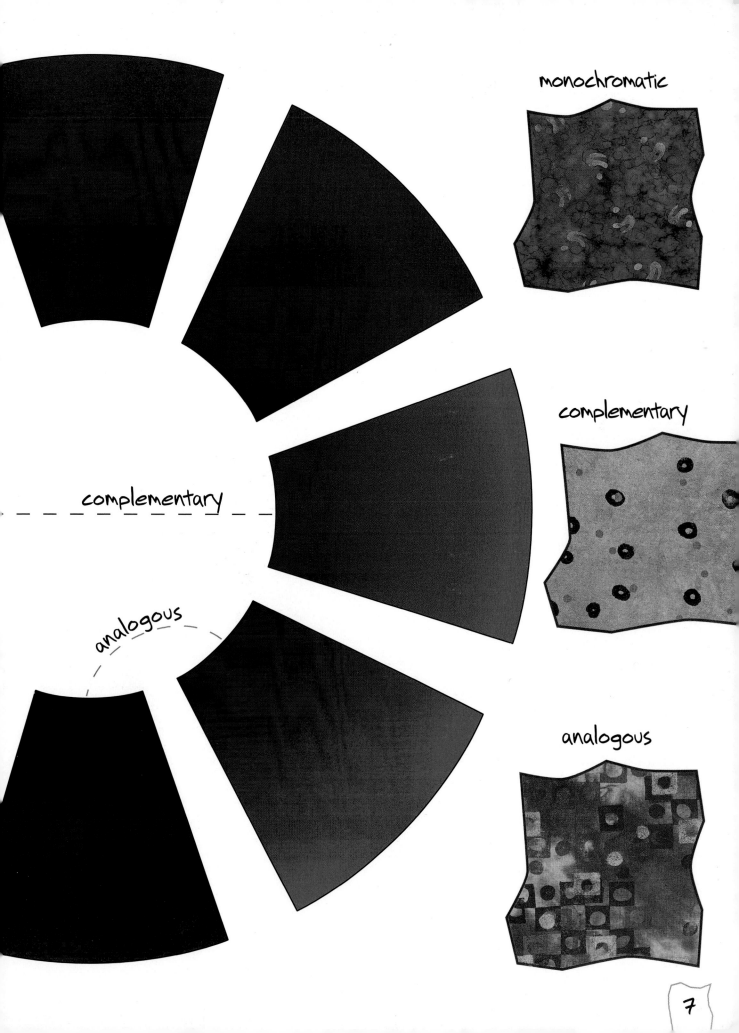

monochromatic

complementary

complementary

analogous

analogous

7

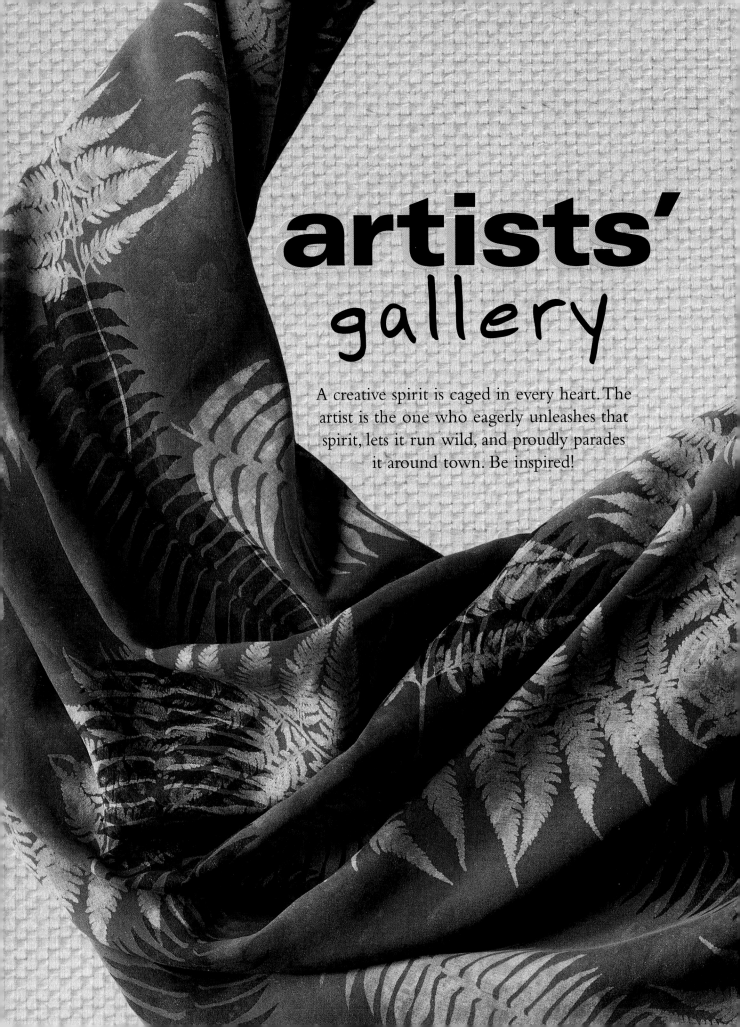

artists'
gallery

A creative spirit is caged in every heart. The artist is the one who eagerly unleashes that spirit, lets it run wild, and proudly parades it around town. Be inspired!

Diane Bartels

Amy Evenson Morris

Amy Evenson Morris spends her days making fiber art and caring for her two children. Her fascination with silk painting and surface design began as a natural outgrowth of a love for other fiber arts, including knitting and quilting. She sells her original designs directly to clients from all over North America. Amy used a metallic gold resist in the serti technique to dye the square silk scarf at left. In the silk crepe de chine scarf, below, she used a combination of techniques with sea salt and alcohol to create the interesting patterns.

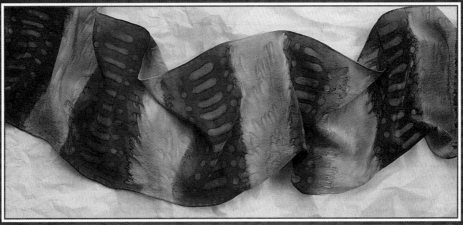

Wendy Richardson

Wendy Richardson has found a niche for herself overdyeing commercially printed fabrics in a low-water immersion process. She sells her visually rich fabrics, garments, patterns, and quiltworks at quilt shows and art fairs around the country and in Europe. Wendy herself is an accomplished quilter; she has won numerous awards and is represented at museums and in private collections.

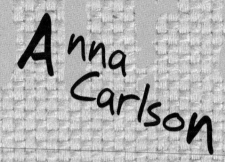

Anna Carlson

Anna Carlson designs, creates, and embellishes coats, jackets, vests, and coordinates that combine beautiful colors and excellence in construction with an artist's sensitivity. She is fascinated by rich and varied surfaces; thus, her work involves the layering of color, piecing, appliqué, and stitching to create surfaces that invite a closer look and a touch. Her garments have simple classic lines that showcase the fabric, embellishments, and impeccable detailing.

Susan Stein

Susan Stein began to explore the world of quilting in 1977. What began as a hobby soon turned into a passion, as Susan charted a path that led her into many roles. She owned two quilt shops in Minnesota, taught both locally and nationally, and served as state guild president. From her current home in Ohio, she sells quilts in two galleries while pursuing her interest in contemporary quilt design and writing a book on innovative Double Wedding Rings. Hand-dyed fabrics are integral to many of her quilt designs. She also incorporates stamping and other painting techniques that give her quilts their one-of-a-kind personality.

Diane Bartels

Diane Bartels has the ability to combine abstraction and reality with color and depth to create fabrics that are admired and cherished for their artistic merits alone. Along with a variety of dyeing methods, she uses a wide range of printing techniques in her textile art: screen printing, stamping, stenciling, and high-tech computer processes. This quilt exhibits some of her less complex, yet artistically fascinating, designs created by sun printing and hand-dyeing. Diane was a major contributor of research for this book. Her fabrics are also shown on pages 8, 34, 35, and 36.

Rebecca Yaffe

Rebecca Yaffe began her art career as a theatrical scene painter, working in several states across the country. Now from Colorado, she owns and operates Rebecca Yaffe Designs, where she designs, dyes, and paints fabrics for clothing and interiors. Her work, shown in galleries and exhibits locally and nationally, includes a line of fabrics created for a private label clothing collection. Shown above are a hand-dyed, hand-painted, and sprayed raw silk shirt and wall covering, and close-up views of Rebecca's hand-dyed, hand-painted jacquard silk scarves.

Laurie Schafer

Laurie Schafer describes her signature technique for creating unique, sumptuous artwear as "stained glass appliqué." Working mainly with silk dupioni, she designs eye-popping appliqué designs on a framework of black fabric. While employing many couture techniques, Laurie adds a personal touch to many of her pieces by embellishing the lining with a song, poem, or message done in gold calligraphy.

Fiona

Peggotty Christensen

Peggotty Christensen's vivid, original garments begin as white silk. With an inspired hand, she creates bold, colorful designs, using fiber-reactive dyes. Many of her designs are influenced by the beauty and tradition of the American Southwest, where she lives. Previously a metalsmith and jewelry designer for 30 years, Peggotty began her transition to textiles in the late 1980s, finding that both mediums shared many of the same design elements. She likens the layering of color on silk to the layering of different metals to create jewelry.

Nancy Eha

Nancy Eha is a nationally known beadwork artist, teacher, and author who encourages participants to go beyond the lure of color, sparkle, and beauty of beadwork, and reflect on the title or subject matter of her art. Many of her beadwork pieces require at least 50 hours of labor, with the goal of being juried into national exhibits. Nancy continually challenges herself to develop new beading techniques, include unusual objects, and provide an element of surprise in every piece.

Natalia Margulis

Natalia Margulis is a native of Russia where, since childhood, she learned and developed skills in all kinds of hand and machine needlework. Her extensive travels and studies of Russian folk arts are the basis for her artistic interpretations of hand embroidery techniques into free-motion machine embroidery. Natalia "paints" thread on fabric, following her own patterns or designing as she stitches. Now an American citizen, her creations have won numerous awards and made her a sought-after teacher.

Penelope Trudeau

Penelope Trudeau creates expressive wall hangings and garments, using various hand-dyeing and painting techniques, adding appliqués, embroidery, and beadwork.

The elaborate network of couched threads and beadwork on this quilt is carefully choreographed to accent and echo the dramatic color dance of the dyes, created by friend and fellow fabric artist, Gail LaLonde. Penelope found the process, though intricate and very time-consuming, to be a thrilling challenge and one of her most creatively satisfying projects.

The hand-dyed, screen-printed silk noile on the cover is another example of Penelope's work.

Julann Windsperger

Julann Windsperger finds time outside of her nursing career to create hand-dyed and painted fabrics which she turns into one-of-a-kind garments like this three-piece ensemble, which won first place at the Minnesota State Fair. It features several immersion-dyed fabrics that are also screen-printed and stamped. The outer vest, made of cotton velveteen, is machine-quilted for added texture.

Susan Frame

Susan Frame utilizes some rather unique methods for painting and dyeing fabric, creating interesting effects using common materials. For instance, the garment shown here was first stamped using a rock from the shore of Lake Superior, dipped in thickened red dye. The surrounding areas were painted with thin dyes and a paintbrush. Susan, who began painting more than 25 years ago, specializes in Sumi-e (Asian brush painting) on rice paper and silk. She has adapted the techniques to silk fabric painting and developed her own couture fashion line.

artists: Jayne Butler

ayne Butler has a passion for fabric sculpture and free-motion machine embroidery. She often incorporates decorative yarns and threads or interesting found objects to create dimension and texture. In the purse at right, she featured a heated and texturized recycled soda can. Throughout her life, sewing has always been a main focus, thanks in great part to her mother, who taught her to sew and encouraged her creativity. In her native Australia, Jayne studied under Dutch couture, Greta Amiet. She is a member of many sewing and machine embroidery organizations and the winner of numerous awards. Jayne shares her knowledge and enthusiasm for creative sewing through her nationwide workshops.

dyeing

AND

design

techniques

Have you ever dreamed of being a textile designer? Simple technology and innovative products to make that dream come true are now at your fingertips. Start exploring!

Penelope Trudeau

Fabrics

Selection and preparation of the fabric you wish to color are two very important steps in the success of your project. There are several things to consider, depending on the techniques and products you intend to use. These include fiber content, weave structure, surface texture, and color.

Fiber-reactive dyes, for instance, are formulated to work well on cellulose fiber, such as cotton, linen, ramie, rayon, tencel, or jute. They also work well on silk, which is a protein fiber. The dyes do not work on synthetic fabrics, though it is possible, but not predictable, to get satisfactory results on fabric blends high in cellulose fibers. Cellulose fibers are also the choice for discharging dye, since bleach has no effect on synthetics, and it damages protein fibers, like wool and silk.

For painting on fabric, the surface texture and tightness of the weave, more than the fiber content, will affect the outcome. Surface texture inherent in the weave of the fabric will naturally affect applications such as stamping, stenciling, or photo transfer. The tighter the weave and smoother the surface, the less the image will be distorted.

You can purchase fabrics that have been prepared for dyeing at some quilt shops, specialty fabric stores, or through mail order sources (page 112). These fabrics are free of any impurities or finishes that would interfere with the dyeing or painting process. They may not, however, have been preshrunk. Avoid permanent-press, stain-repellent, or water-resistant finishes. These finishes, which will inhibit dyes from bonding or paints from adhering, are extremely difficult to remove. To prepare other fabric for dyeing or painting, wash it in hot water with Synthrapol® (page 29) and soda ash (page 29), using ¼ teaspoon (1 mL) of each per yard (0.95 m) of fabric. Do not use fabric softener in either the washer or dryer.

Julann Windsperger

Amy Morris

Lastly, consider the fabric's color. Dyes, some paints, and photo transfers are transparent, so the base color of the fabric will affect the coloring process. White fabric is essential if you want to dye fabric to match a color card. Even unbleached muslin adds a yellow element to the outcome. Dark and bright colors work best for discharging. White or pastels are recommended for photo transfers.

Occasionally some great finds are discovered in remnant piles, and the fabric may not be labeled. If you are unsure of the fiber content, ravel off a few yarns, roll them into a ball, and hold them with tweezers as you burn them. Compare the results to the descriptions, right. If you are a fabric stockpiler, as many of us are, be sure to label the fabrics you buy with information about specific fiber content, finishes, and whether or not it has been prepared for dyeing. You'll eliminate some guesswork, trial, and error later on.

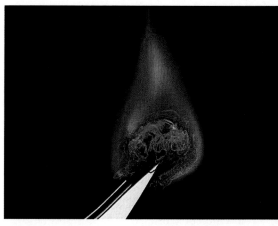

Cotton, linen, and rayon fibers burn vigorously, with an afterglow. They burn with the odor of burning paper and leave a soft, gray ash.

Wool and silk fibers burn slowly and char, curling away from the flame. They sometimes burn only while in the flame. They burn with the odor of burning hair or feathers and leave a crushable ash.

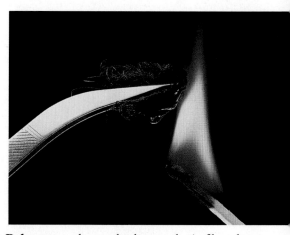

Polyester, nylon, and other synthetic fibers burn and melt only while in the flame, or shortly after being removed. They burn with a chemical odor and leave a hard bead.

28

Fabric dyes give you the capability of achieving rich brilliant color, subtle shading and highlighting, and watercolor blended effects without changing the hand of the fabric. Browse through mail-order catalogs and you will find a wide assortment of dyes in powder or liquid form, some developed for specific techniques and others versatile enough to be used for almost anything. There are even dyes available in crayon and marker forms, putting instant color capability at your fingertips. Read the manufacturer's directions and experiment with different forms and brands to discover your own favorites.

One of the most popular dyes is Procion® MX, a fiber-reactive powdered dye, mixed and used at room temperature. It is formulated for dyeing natural-fiber fabrics: cotton, rayon, silk, or wool. The term "fiber-reactive" means that during the dyeing process, a chemical reaction occurs, permanently bonding the dye molecules with the fiber molecules. In essence, the dye becomes part of the fabric. This results in brilliant color that cannot wash out or rub off.

Along with the dye powders and water, there are a few other products necessary to mix and use fiber-reactive dyes. *Synthrapol,* used to prewash fabric to remove any sizing, dirt, or other impurities that would inhibit dyeing, is also used in the final wash to remove any loose dye particles. *Soda ash fixer*, commonly known as sodium carbonate, is a mild alkali that facilitates the chemical reaction between the dye and the fibers. *Urea* is an organic nitrogen that keeps the fabric wetter longer, allowing the chemical reaction to take place. *Calsolene oil* is a liquid wetting agent that increases the saturation power of the water and consequently the dye. A thickener, called PRO Print Paste Mix SH, available from PRO Chemical and Dye, Inc. (page 112) can be added to the dye to make it suitable for direct applications, like stamping or screen printing.

Dyeing methods include *immersion,* used when you want to dye a piece of fabric all one color, and *low-water immersion,* which results in a one-color or multicolor textured look with variations in value. Low-water immersion can also be used to overdye printed fabrics. Fabric dyed with either of these methods provides a wonderful canvas for further color and design work, including *direct dye application,* where multiple dye colors can be applied in a variety of methods and consistencies. In immersion dyeing, the soda ash is added to the dye bath, activating the chemical reaction. For direct application methods, the fabric is presoaked in the soda ash water, and either hung to dry or spread out damp or wet for applying the dye. The chemical reaction begins when the dye touches the fabric in the presence of the soda ash.

For most applications, the dye powder is first mixed with water in a concentrated form. The recipes and directions that follow are only general guidelines. Dye manufacturers provide information for determining the amount of dye powder required to dye specific amounts of fabric to match each color in their color cards. Keep a detailed notebook of the recipes and dyelots used in each dyeing session, if you want to be able to repeat hues, values, and intensities.

Though the Procion dyes are nontoxic, certain precautions should be taken when using them. Always wear a dust mask when mixing the dye to avoid inhaling the powder. Wear rubber gloves and use utensils and containers for mixing and storing dyes that will not be used for food. Keep all mixtures well-labeled and away from children and pets. Unused dye mixtures or exhausted dye baths can safely be poured down the drain without harming the environment.

■ ■ ■ ■ ■ ■ ■ ■ ■ ■ ■ Immersion Dyeing ■ ■ ■ ■ ■ ■ ■ ■ ■ ■ ■

MATERIALS

- ❏ Natural-fiber fabric, prepared for dyeing (page 26); up to 3 yd. (2.75 m).
- ❏ Washing machine; dryer.
- ❏ Large plastic bucket; wooden or plastic mixing spoons.
- ❏ Rubber gloves; dust mask.
- ❏ 1½ gallons (5.75 L) water.

- ❏ 1½ cups (375 mL) noniodized salt.
- ❏ Procion MX fiber-reactive dye powder (2 to 8 teaspoons per 1 lb. [10 to 40 mL per 500 g] of dry fabric, according to manufacturer's recommendations).
- ❏ Soda ash; water.
- ❏ 1 teaspoon (5 mL) Calsolene oil.
- ❏ Synthrapol.

1 Prepare fabric for dyeing (page 26). Dissolve salt in lukewarm water in large bucket; add Calsolene oil. Dissolve dye completely in 1 cup (250 mL) of warm water; add to bucket, and stir to distribute evenly. In separate container, prepare soda bath (below); set aside.

2 Put thoroughly wet fabric into dye bath. Stir fabric almost constantly for 20 minutes. Pour 2 cups (500 mL) soda bath, small amounts at a time, into dye bath, stirring constantly; avoid pouring directly onto fabric. Allow fabric to remain in dye bath ½ hour to 1 hour, depending on color intensity desired; stir occasionally.

3 Remove fabric, pour dye bath down drain; it is not reusable. Set machine for warm wash/warm rinse; put fabric in filled machine, and allow to run through cycle. Reset machine for hot wash/warm rinse, add Synthrapol (¼ teaspoon [1 mL] per yard [0.95 m] of fabric), and wash. Machine dry.

Soda Bath

1 cup (250 mL) soda ash
1 gallon (3.8 L) hot water

Mix until completely dissolved; allow to cool to room temperature.

Dye Concentrate

2½ tablespoons (37.5 mL) urea
½ cup (125 mL) warm water
1 tablespoon (15 mL) dye powder

Mix well. Label and store in refrigerator when not in use.

Dye Concentrate to Water Ratios

Dark: 6 tablespoons to 10 tablespoons (90 to 150 mL)

Medium: 3 tablespoons to 13 tablespoons (45 to 195 mL)

Light: 1 tablespoon to 15 tablespoons (15 to 225 mL)

Pour dye concentrate in measuring cup; add water to make 1 cup (250 mL).

M A T E R I A L S

- ❏ Natural-fiber fabric, prepared for dyeing (page 26); up to 3 yd. (2.75 m).
- ❏ Washing machine; dryer.
- ❏ Large plastic bucket.
- ❏ Large plastic vat or dishpan; wooden or plastic mixing spoons.
- ❏ Rubber gloves; dust mask.
- ❏ 1½ gallons (5.75 L) water.

- ❏ 1½ cups (375 mL) noniodized salt.
- ❏ Procion MX fiber-reactive dye powder (2 to 8 teaspoons per 1 lb. [10 to 40 mL per 500 g] of dry fabric, according to manufacturer's recommendations).
- ❏ ⅙ cup (42 mL) soda ash.
- ❏ 1 teaspoon (5 mL) Calsolene oil.

1 Prepare fabric for dyeing (page 26); tear into manageable pieces, ½ yd. to 1½ yd. (0.5 to 1.4 m). Dissolve salt in lukewarm water in large bucket; immerse fabric. In separate container, prepare soda bath (opposite). Prepare dye concentrates (opposite).

2 Remove fabric from salt water; wring out excess. Arrange single layer of fabric in bottom of vat; scrunch as necessary to fit. Dilute dye concentrate with water following ratio guide, opposite. Pour over fabric, distributing evenly; use 1 to 2 cups (250 to 500 mL), depending on amount and thickness of fabric. Allow to sit for 10 to 15 minutes.

3 Pour soda bath over fabric, using about half as much soda bath as you used of dye mixture; distribute evenly. Allow to sit for 1½ hours. Remove fabric from vat; pour dye mixture down drain. Rinse and wash fabric as in step 3, opposite.

MATERIALS

- Natural-fiber fabric, prepared for dyeing (page 26).
- Plastic drop cloth; large plastic plates.
- Procion MX fiber-reactive dyes, in desired colors.
- Urea.
- Soda ash.
- Synthropol.
- String, rubber bands, or clothespins, for "tying" fabrics.
- Measuring spoons, cups, plastic spoons, for mixing dyes.
- Rubber gloves; face mask.
- Zip-lock plastic bags.

Thickened Dye

5½ tablespoons (82.5 mL) PRO Print Mix SH

1 cup (250 mL) water

Add print mix slowly to water, stirring constantly. Thin, if desired, adding urea water (7 teaspoons. [35 mL] urea to 1 cup [250 mL] water) in small amounts. Allow to sit overnight. Mix equal parts with dye concentrate, for dark value. Adjust ratio for lighter values. Mix only as much as you will use in one session.

1 Mix thickened dye (above) as necessary for technique. Prepare fabric for dyeing (page 26). Immerse fabric in soda bath (page 30); allow to soak for 20 minutes. Remove fabric; wring out excess water. Hang to dry or use wet or damp as technique requires.

2 Cover work surface with plastic drop cloth. Spread fabric on surface; secure with tape or T-pins. Apply dye to fabric using paintbrush, foam applicator, roller, or other technique, such as stamping (page 36), stenciling (page 42), or screen printing (page 46). Cover fabric with sheet of plastic. Roll up layers, and allow fabric to cure at room temperature for at least 24 hours.

3 Unroll fabric; remove plastic. Rinse in cool water, then warm water, gradually changing to hot water, until water runs clear. Machine wash, using Synthropol; machine dry.

Silk dyes. Stretch silk on wooden frame. Apply liquid silk dyes in desired colors and pattern; allow to dry. Apply rubbing alcohol in desired areas to create highlights; use paintbrush, foam applicator, or cotton swab, or drip alcohol on silk. Allow reaction to take place; dry. Steam-set (page 61).

Dye sticks and markers. Draw directly on fabric, using dye sticks or markers. Overlap colors to blend. Shade a color, using its complementary color (page 6). Allow to dry. Heat-set, following manufacturer's directions.

Fabric Paints

Painting is one of the easiest methods of putting color and design on fabric. Fabric paints are basically pigments attached to binders or adhesives. When you paint on fabric, the binders adhere the pigments to the fibers. Fabric paints may change the hand of the fabric in varying degrees, depending on the brand, type, and consistency of the paint you use.

Fabric paints are available in both opaque and transparent types. Transparent paints allow the fabric's print or color to show through, and are suitable anytime you want a sheer, color-washed look. Opaques cover the surface completely, making them ideal for painting on dark or black fabric. Pearlized or metallic paints dry with a lustrous appearance.

Paints can be used in their natural consistency or diluted with water. There are various consistencies available, each suited to particular application techniques. For instance, paints suitable for screen printing have the consistency of pudding; those used for painting on silk are like water.

Methods for Painting on Fabric

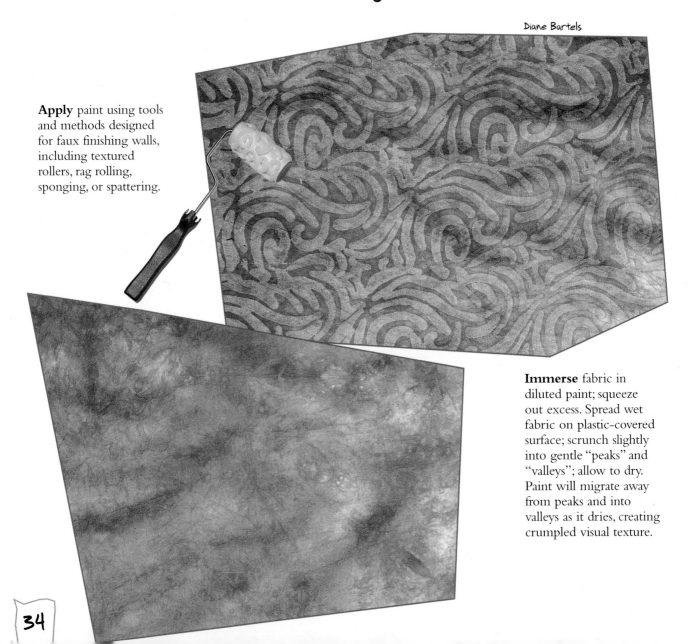

Diane Bartels

Apply paint using tools and methods designed for faux finishing walls, including textured rollers, rag rolling, sponging, or spattering.

Immerse fabric in diluted paint; squeeze out excess. Spread wet fabric on plastic-covered surface; scrunch slightly into gentle "peaks" and "valleys"; allow to dry. Paint will migrate away from peaks and into valleys as it dries, creating crumpled visual texture.

Aside from the specific techniques of stamping (page 36), stenciling (page 42), and screen printing (page 46), paints can be applied to fabric in countless ways. Experiment with paintbrushes, rollers, foam applicators, sponges, feathers, fingers, syringes, sprayers, or any method imaginable. For ease in application, tape fabric to a slightly padded surface, protected with a plastic drop cloth.

Natural-fiber fabrics are recommended for painting techniques, though some synthetic blends are suitable also, as long as they can withstand the high heat necessary to set the paint. Prewashing the fabric in hot water and mild detergent removes any sizing that may have been applied during manufacturing, optimizing the paint's ability to adhere to the fibers. Twenty-four hours after air-drying, heat-set the painted fabric, pressing with a dry iron from the wrong side or using a press cloth. Though fabric paints can be dry-cleaned and are fade-resistant, they may rub off with repeated washing or friction, so wash gently to preserve the color and design.

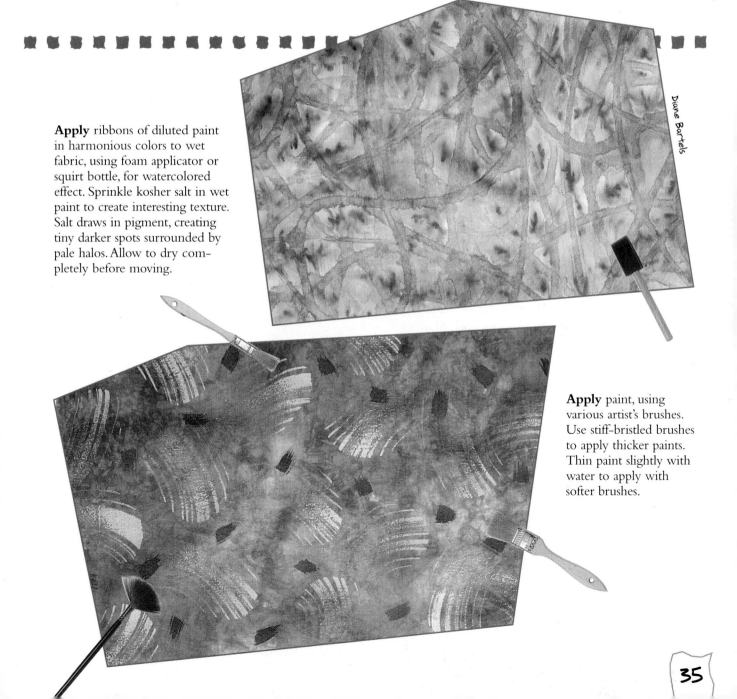

Apply ribbons of diluted paint in harmonious colors to wet fabric, using foam applicator or squirt bottle, for watercolored effect. Sprinkle kosher salt in wet paint to create interesting texture. Salt draws in pigment, creating tiny darker spots surrounded by pale halos. Allow to dry completely before moving.

Diane Bartels

Apply paint, using various artist's brushes. Use stiff-bristled brushes to apply thicker paints. Thin paint slightly with water to apply with softer brushes.

Stamping

With a little imagination, many household items become tools for stamping designs on fabric. Try a wooden spaghetti lifter, flat metal hardware items, plastic bubble wrap, or a ball of string. Small objects, such as buttons, coins, or keys, can be glued to the end of a wooden dowel, empty film container, or large cork for easy stamping. In fact, cork itself can be cut into interesting shapes for printing fabric. Some items are more easily used for stamping if they are not mounted to a surface. Cellulose sponges cut into shapes produce wonderful textured effects. Leaves, flower petals, or grasses may be used to produce whispy, nature prints. And don't forget your vegetables!

Purchased stamps, particularly those with less fine detail work, are also useful for stamping on fabric. Printing blocks can be cut from a number of materials, including white artist's erasers or larger blocks made of the same material, available at art supply stores. These blocks are easily cut with a mat knife or linoleum block cutters. Any closed cell foam material, including neoprene sheets, insulation tapes, or computer mouse pads can be cut into shapes with scissors and attached to a block for printing. Art supply stores also carry adhesive-backed sheets of closed cell foam, designed for this purpose.

The weave structure of the fabric plays a large part in the clarity of the printing. Obviously, the clearest results are obtained on tightly woven fabric with fine yarns. The looser the weave and the larger the yarns, the more distorted the stamped image will be.

Use any fabric paints, inks, or dyes to stamp the images on fabric. Also, use this stamping technique for applying resists (page 50) or for discharging dye (page 67) to create a stamped image. Follow the manufacturers' directions for using the products and for setting the stamped images permanently in the fabric.

Diane Bartels

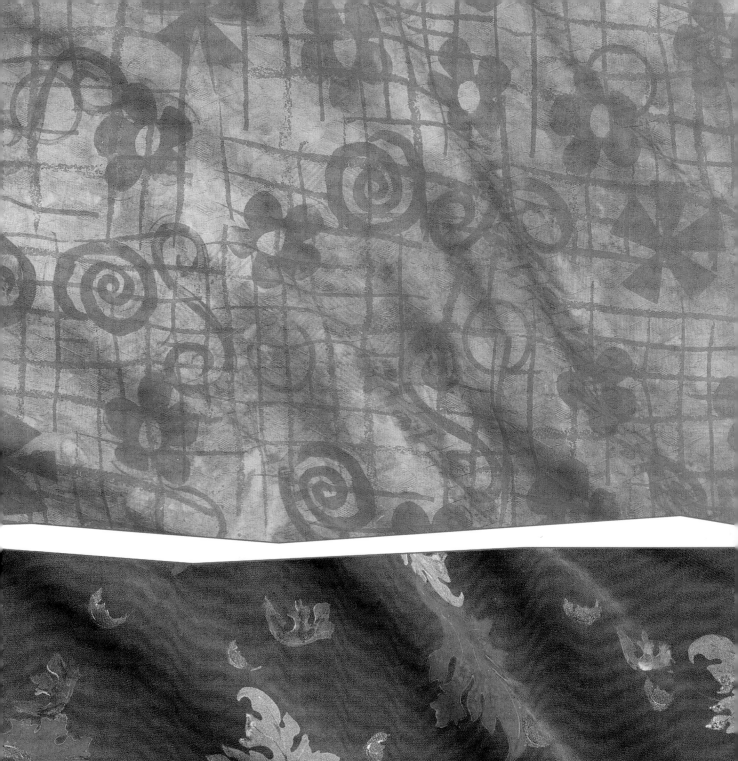

Secure small items such as coins, buttons, or metal washers to dowel ends, bottle corks, or empty film containers, using silicone glue.

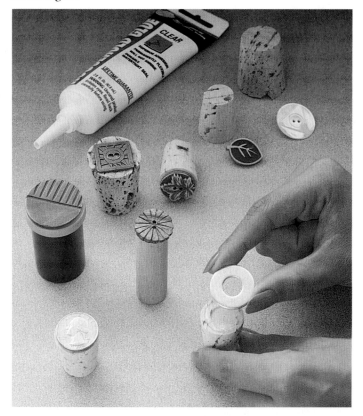

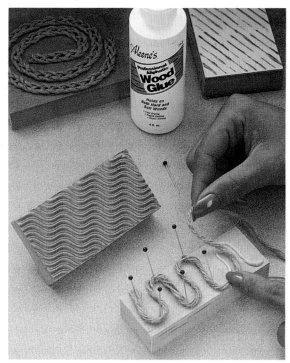

Spread wood glue on wood block. Arrange uniform layer of rope, cording, or string in desired design in wet glue; allow to dry. Or secure ribbed fabric, corrugated cardboard, or other textural material. Print design on paper; adhere to top of block, to aid in positioning stamp.

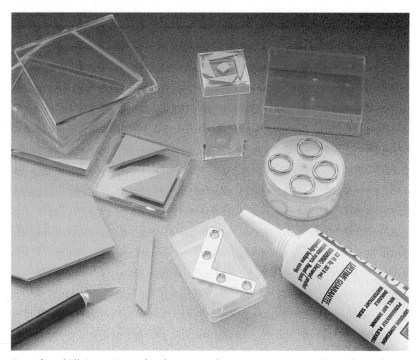

Cut clear ¼" (6 mm) acrylic sheet into shapes or use empty clear plastic boxes in assorted sizes for see-through printing blocks. Cut layered self-adhesive foam into desired shapes; mount to blocks. Mount other items using silicone glue.

1 Draw design on surface of block material or transfer design to surface using transfer paper. Cut about ¼" (6 mm) deep into block along outer design lines, using mat knife.

2 Remove large background area around design by cutting horizontally through edge of block up to cuts made for design outline.

3 Cut and remove negative areas within design, cutting at an angle along each edge.

Linoleum cutter method. Carve away negative areas of design, using linoleum cutting tools. Follow manufacturer's directions for using tools. Some styles are pushed to cut; others are pulled.

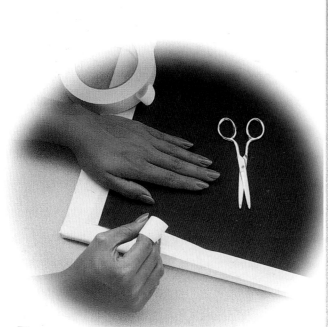

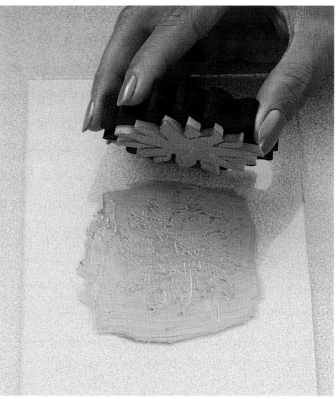

Place fabric to be stamped over smooth, padded surface, such as muslin layered over foam-core board. Stretch taut, and secure with masking tape around edges.

Apply thin layer of fabric paint to smooth surface, such as sheet of glass. Press stamping material onto surface to pick up paint for stamping. Recoat surface as needed.

Apply paint or ink directly onto stamping surface, using foam applicator. This allows you to print multicolored designs.

Make a stamp pad by placing several layers of felt on a smooth, flat surface; thoroughly wet, but do not saturate, felt with fabric dye, ink, or thinned paint (four parts paint to one part extender). Press printing block evenly into felt pad, lightly coating surface. Stamp fabric.

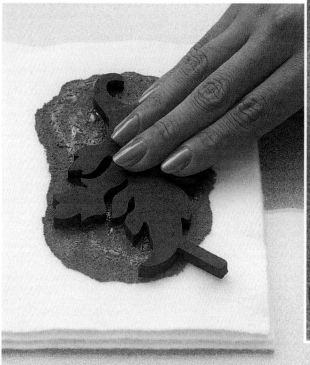

Reapply dye, ink, or paint after each stamp for designs of relatively same intensity.

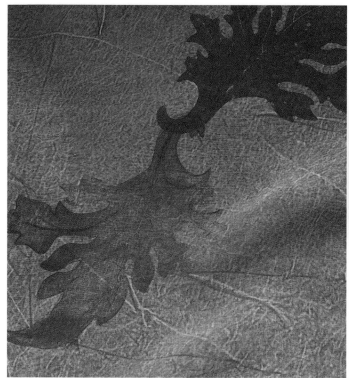

Brush paint onto uncut surface of artist's eraser or printing block. Remove paint to create a negative design, using a wipe out tool, pencil eraser, or corner of another artist's eraser. Print design onto fabric.

Stamp two or three times before reapplying paint or ink for designs with varying intensities, depth, and shading.

Stenciling

Stenciling produces single or repeated designs with gradations of color. A multitude of commercial stencils is available. Most commercial stencils have separate stencil plates for each color, numbered according to sequence of use. For stenciling fabric, avoid stencils with minute details that will be distorted or lost by the fabric grain. You may choose to design and make your own stencils or copy a design from another source, altering the size as needed.

Stenciling is a very versatile technique, suitable for a wide range of mediums, including fabric paints, dye sticks, resists, and bleach. With proper care and storage, stencils will last a long time.

Materials

❑ Colored pencils; paper.
❑ Transparent Mylar® sheets.
❑ Fine-point permanent marker.
❑ Mat knife; cutting surface, such as self-healing cutting board.

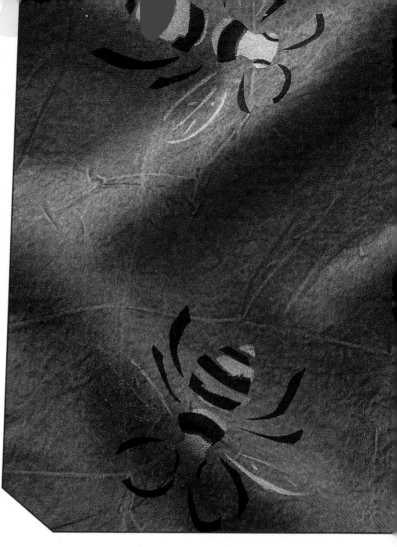

How to Make a Custom Stencil

1 Draw or trace design; color in areas of design to be cut out, using colored pencils. If multiple plates are desired, color areas for each plate a different color. Mark placement guides.

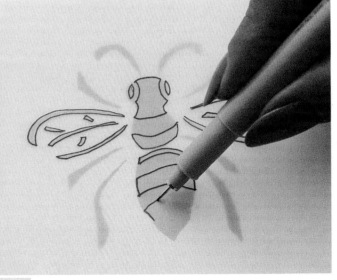

2 Position Mylar sheet over traced design, allowing at least 1" (2.5 cm) border at top and bottom; secure with tape. Trace areas to be stenciled in first color, using marking pen. Transfer placement guides.

3 Trace design areas for each additional color on separate Mylar sheets; transfer placement guides on each sheet. Layer sheets to check for accuracy.

4 Cut out marked designs on each sheet, using mat knife. Pull knife toward you as you cut, turning sheet, rather than knife, to change direction.

Use stencil brush or foam applicator in size appropriate for stencil openings. Apply medium with dabbing or pouncing motion. Brushing motion may cause medium to leak under edges of opening.

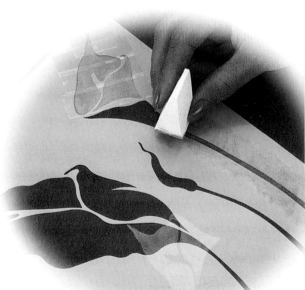

Mask off openings as necessary, if more than one color will be applied using the same stencil plate.

Overlap stenciled images to create depth. Allow first layer to dry before stenciling second layer.

Apply repositionable spray adhesive to back of stencil to help it stick to fabric.

Vary the stenciled effect by using other tools to apply paint, such as sea sponge, cellulose sponge, or spray applicator.

Clean stencils thoroughly immediately after each use. Lay stencil flat; dab with wet sponge. Do not rub or brush. Allow to dry. Repair minor tears in the stencil with cellophane tape.

Screen Printing

Screen printing is another method for printing single or repeating images. Unlike the gradated and shaded images produced by stenciling, and the characteristic inconsistent images produced by stamping, screen-printed images feature crisp lines and total, even coverage. In this method, the design is prepared on a fine mesh screen using water-soluble Speedball® Screen Drawing Fluid and Screen Filler. The coloring medium is forced through the mesh with a squeegee, printing the fabric in the open areas of the design.

Art supply stores and mail order companies carry convenient ready-made printing screens in a variety of sizes. The screen consists of a wooden frame with finely woven fabric (silk or polyester) stretched tautly across one side. The mesh is sized according to the openness of the weave; the smaller the number, the more open the weave. Purchase multifilament polyester screens with 12xx mesh.

Water-based textile inks, created for screen printing, are used most often, though thickened dye and most fabric paints can be used also. For best results, the medium must have the consistency of pudding. Avoid paints that contain glitter, as the glitter will clog the screen. Besides printing images onto fabric, the screen printing method can also be used for discharging dye (page 67) from fabric or for applying a resist (page 50).

For best results, work on a smooth padded surface. Secure foam rubber and batting, several layers of muslin, or terry cloth to a large board and stretch muslin or an old sheet over it, making certain there are no wrinkles in the layers.

MATERIALS

❏ Printing screen with 12xx multifilament polyester mesh in desired size.

❏ Duct tape.

❏ Speedball Water-soluble Screen Drawing Fluid and Screen Filler.

❏ Textile inks, textile paints, or thickened dye.

❏ Squeegee, ½" (1.3 cm) narrower than inside measurement of screen frame.

❏ Plastic drop cloth; padded work surface; paper towels.

❏ Fabric, prewashed and pressed.

1 Wrap duct tape over all edges of wooden frame to waterproof it. Extend duct tape about ½" (1.3 cm) onto mesh on upper side of screen, forming a border or trough.

2 Elevate screen slightly off work surface. Position design pattern on surface under screen, if desired. Apply screen drawing fluid to mesh in areas you wish to print, using paintbrush or sponge applicator. Allow to dry completely.

3 Apply thin even coat of screen filler over entire screen, using squeegee as on page 48, steps 1 and 2. Allow to dry.

4 Spray cold water on both sides of screen, concentrating on areas where drawing fluid was applied. Screen filler will wash away in these areas; scrub lightly with small stiff brush, if necessary. Allow screen to dry thoroughly.

1 Secure plastic drop cloth tautly over padded work surface. Tautly secure fabric, right side up, over surface. Place screen over fabric. Place 2 to 3 tablespoons (30 to 45 mL) of print medium next to design area or along border.

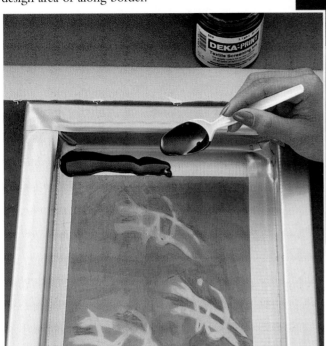

2 Press screen firmly against fabric with one hand. Applying firm, even pressure, pull squeegee across the screen, drawing medium across open areas of design. Hold squeegee at an angle, leaning in the direction you are pulling it. Scoop up excess paint with squeegee; deposit at top of screen. Repeat motion until medium is evenly distributed.

3 Lift screen slowly from fabric at an angle. Reposition screen and repeat process in another area, if desired. Avoid placing screen over wet medium. Work quickly so that medium does not dry on screen.

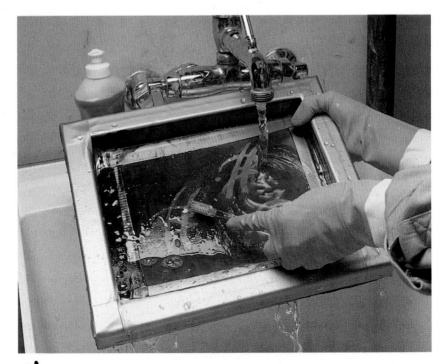

4 Wash screen with soap under warm running water immediately after printing. Dry screen completely before using again. Touch up blocked area with screen filler as necessary.

Allow screen-printed images to dry completely before printing over them a second time or before printing right next to them, so that frame of screen does not smudge adjacent images.

Apply two or more colors of ink or paint next to each other along the top of the screen to print an image with a blended color effect.

Screen print images over dry fabric that has been discharged (page 67), dyed, or painted with another technique, to create depth.

Prepare a separate screen for each design and color you wish to print to minimize the total printing time required. Print all of one color or design, and wash screen before proceeding to next screen.

49

Resists

Mechanical Resists

1. Arrange items, such as leaves, buttons, wooden shapes, doilies, decorator trim, or anything that will provide interesting shape over surface of fabric. Dilute fabric paint to milky consistency; pour into household spray bottle. Spray paint over fabric in thin coats, allowing fabric to dry between coats. Angle of spray may create shadow effect behind resist object. Remove items; heat-set.

2. Fold, crumple, twist, stitch, or tie off fabric with rubber bands as for tie-dyeing (page 52). Apply diluted fabric paint; allow to dry. Smooth out fabric, and heat-set. Or prepare resist and apply bleach solution, using tie-dye methods; follow page 68, steps 1 to 3, to discharge dye in unique pattern.

3. Apply masking tape to fabric surface in desired design. Or cut a design from self-adhesive vinyl, and apply to fabric. Brush or spray fabric paint over surface of fabric. Allow to dry completely before removing resist; heat-set. This method creates sharply defined lines.

Just as the name implies, a resist is a means of creating a design by enabling the fabric to resist a dye, paint, or discharge solution. The design results from the negative colored space. Some resists are mechanical, meaning something is placed over the fabric or the fabric is manipulated in a way to prevent color medium from reaching certain areas. Leaves, paper doilies, or a plastic comb placed on the surface of the fabric to block sprayed paint, dye, or bleach are simple mechanical resists. Another common mechanical resist method is to fold, twist, or otherwise manipulate the fabric, securing it with rubber bands, clamps, or strings, thus prohibiting the color medium from reaching certain parts of the fabric.

Water-based resists are substances that temporarily coat the fibers, prohibiting them from accepting the color medium. These liquid resists are applied to the fabric by any means also suitable for fabric paint, thickened dyes, or bleach gel. They must be thoroughly dry to be effective, preferably for twenty-four hours. Because they are water-soluble, they are not suitable for coloring methods that wet the fabric, such as immersion dyeing. After painting or dyeing, the resist washes out, leaving a negative design (positive, when discharging). Water-based resists are available from art supply stores and catalogs. Follow the manufacturers' directions for specific use of their products.

The examples (right) were prepared using fabric paints. Similar effects can be created by direct application of dyes (page 32) over resists.

Water-based Resists

4. Apply water-based resist to rubber stamp or other item used for stamping; stamp fabric. Reapply resist after ever stamp. Allow resist to dry thoroughly. Apply fabric paint over stamped designs, using desired method. Allow to dry. Heat-set paint. Wash fabric to remove resist.

5. Apply water-based resist to fabric, using paintbrush, for broad strokes and large, filled-in areas. Use fine-tipped dispenser for applying narrow lines or handwriting. Allow to dry thoroughly. Paint fabric as desired; heat-set. Wash fabric to remove resist.

6. Apply resist, using screen-printing method, page 46. Allow to dry thoroughly. Apply fabric paint over screen-printed designs, using desired method. Allow to dry. Heat-set paint. Wash fabric to remove resist.

Tie-dyeing

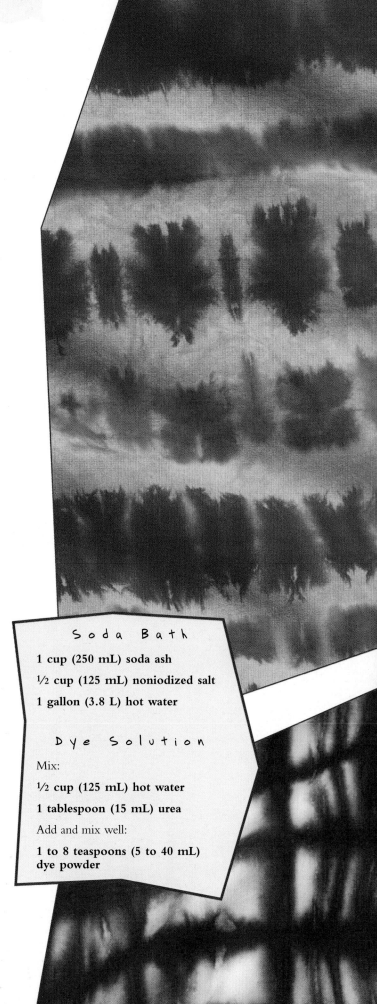

All the rage in the '60s and still going strong, tie-dyeing is an everpopular method of obtaining vivid colorful designs on fabric. It's not just for T-shirts anymore, either. Quilters and garment artisans alike take advantage of the color explosions, patterning, and visual depth of tie-dyed fabric.

In simplest terms, tie-dyeing involves the manipulation of fabric by folding, twisting, scrunching, or stitching to create a resist (page 50) in certain areas, blocking them from receiving dye. Rubber bands, string, or clothespins are used to hold the manipulated fabric in place. In the direct application method taught here, dye is applied to the fabric by dipping, squirting, sponging, or brushing, depending on the desired effect.

The best tie-dyed results are achieved using 100% cotton or silk fabric that has been prepared for dyeing (page 26). Other natural fiber fabrics, like rayon and linen, can also be used. Work with manageable pieces, ½ yd. to 1 yd. (0.5 to 0.95 m) square, depending on the manner in which you intend to manipulate the fabric.

Review the information on color (page 6) to help you create combinations that work well together. Be aware that if you apply two complementary colors of dye right next to each other, the fabric may turn brown where the dyes overlap. Some secondary and tertiary colors of dye will produce a halo effect when their component colors penetrate the fabric at different rates. For instance, the blue component of a purple dye may separate out and spread farther into the fabric than the red component, creating a wonderful gradation from red to purple to blue. Experiment with different manipulations and dye combinations, and record your results, but don't be surprised if you have difficulty duplicating favorites.

MATERIALS

- ❏ 100% cotton or silk fabric, prepared for dyeing (page 26).
- ❏ Plastic drop cloth; large plastic plates.
- ❏ Procion MX fiber-reactive dyes, in desired colors.
- ❏ Urea.
- ❏ Soda ash.
- ❏ Salt (canning or pickling).
- ❏ Synthropol.
- ❏ String, rubber bands, or clothespins for "tying" fabrics.
- ❏ Measuring spoons, cups, plastic spoons, for mixing dyes.
- ❏ Rubber gloves; face mask.
- ❏ Zip-lock plastic bags.

Soda Bath

1 cup (250 mL) soda ash

½ cup (125 mL) noniodized salt

1 gallon (3.8 L) hot water

Dye Solution

Mix:

½ cup (125 mL) hot water

1 tablespoon (15 mL) urea

Add and mix well:

1 to 8 teaspoons (5 to 40 mL) dye powder

2 Mix dyes while fabric is soaking. Wear face mask to avoid breathing dye powder; wear rubber gloves.

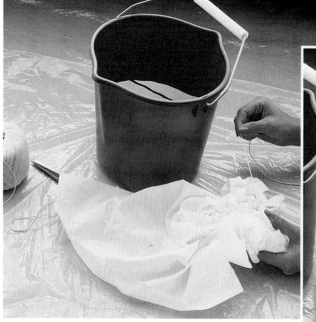

1 Cover work surface with plastic drop cloth. Manipulate fabric as desired; tie or clamp, using rubber bands, string, or clothespins (pages 56 and 57). Prepare soda bath; soak fabric until saturated, about 20 minutes. Gently squeeze excess solution from fabric, but do not rinse.

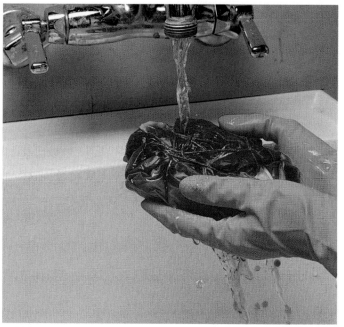

3 Place fabric on large plastic plate. Apply dye to fabric, using desired method (opposite); apply enough dye to penetrate fabric but not puddle on plate. Place tied, dyed fabric into plastic bag; close securely. Allow fabric to cure at room temperature 24 hours.

4 Remove fabric; rinse under running water until water is nearly clear. Untie fabric and rinse again. Wash by hand or machine, using ¼ teaspoon (1 mL) Synthropol per yard (0.95 m) of fabric; final rinse water should be clear. Hang to dry or machine dry. Fabric is colorfast and ready to use.

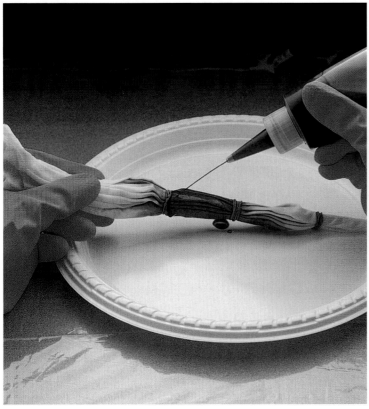

Dipping. Pour dye into shallow, wide bowl. Dip desired area of tied fabric into dye; allow excess dye to drip back into bowl.

Squirt bottle. Pour dye into squirt bottle, using funnel. Squirt dye on fabric in desired areas. Work tip of bottle into folds and crevices.

Foam applicator. Dip foam applicator into dye; brush onto fabric.

Rolled plaid. Fanfold fabric. Roll folded strip into fairly tight circle; tie. Apply dye to one flat side of circle; turn over and apply dye to other side. Use two different colors, if desired.

Stripes. Fanfold fabric. Crease folds if sharp lines are desired. Tie tightly with string or rubber bands at even or uneven intervals. Apply dye to fabric between ties. To dye a plaid pattern, complete page 54, steps 1 to 4, in stripe pattern. Then repeat, folding in opposite direction.

Fanfolded plaid. Fanfold fabric in one direction. Fanfold folded strip in opposite direction. Tie folded stack. Apply dye to folds around outer edges of stack.

Squares and triangles. Fanfold fabric in one direction. Fanfold folded strip in diagonal folds, forming triangular stack; tie. Apply dye to folds around outer edge of stack.

Scrunch. Lay fabric out flat on surface. Beginning at center, scrunch fabric into a shapeless, lumpy wad; tie securely. Apply dye randomly over all exposed surfaces.

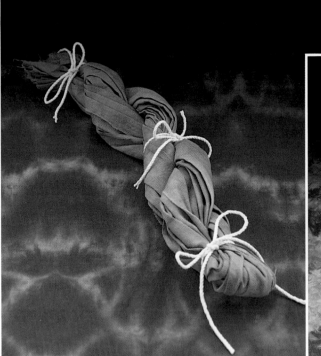

Spiral twist. Loosely scrunch fabric length from one side to the other. Twist ends in opposite directions until fabric doubles over at center; tie. Apply dye randomly over all exposed surfaces.

Starburst. Fold fabric in half; mark center of fold. Beginning at fold, fanfold both layers together in triangular wedges radiating from center of fold; tie in several places from point to ends. Apply dye, alternating colors on folds and flat surfaces.

Gathering stitches. Stitch rows of basting stitches in desired pattern through fabric; use sturdy thread. Pull threads to gather; tie. Apply dye to exposed surfaces.

Serti

Serti is a resist technique that allows you to create dyed designs with distinct, hard lines. Most often used on lightweight China silk, but applicable to other fabrics, serti prevents the blending of the dyes from one area to the next by completely enclosing each design area with a thin line of resist. When applied to the silk, the dye spreads up to the resist, filling in the enclosed space, but going no farther. Brilliant color is best heat-set into the fabric, using a steaming method. After setting the dyed design, the resist is removed, leaving thin white or colored lines between distinct design areas.

Water-based resist, such as Silkpaint!® Resist, is tintable with dyes and easily removed with cool water. It is applied as a liquid, using a fine-tipped applicator squeeze bottle or a convenient tool, called The Airpen®, by Silkpaint Corporation.

The design you create or select should have distinct areas that can be completely enclosed by the resist. It may have additional accent lines that can also be covered with resist.

Materials

- ❏ Lightweight China silk, prepared for dyeing (page 26).
- ❏ Stretcher bar frame and silk tacks or push pins, or large wooden embroidery hoop.
- ❏ Wooden blocks for raising frame.
- ❏ Water-soluble resist.
- ❏ The Airpen, or fine-tipped applicator squeeze bottle.
- ❏ Silk dyes.
- ❏ Soft brushes or foam applicators, for applying dye.
- ❏ Unprinted newsprint; rubber bands.
- ❏ Deep kettle, steaming net or rack, terry towel, aluminum foil, for steaming fabric.

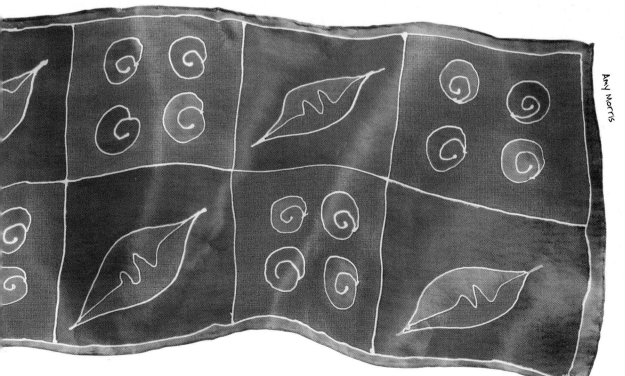

Amy Morris

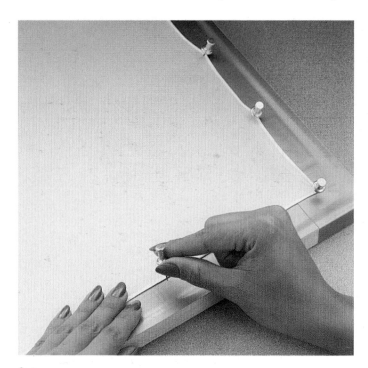

2 Place pattern on table, under silk. Add dye to resist, if color is desired. Pour resist into Airpen or applicator bottle. Apply resist to all design lines, following tips on page 62. Begin in one upper corner and work toward bottom of design to avoid smudging lines.

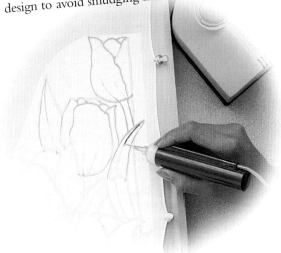

1 Wrap frame with duct tape to protect wood from dyes. Tack silk fabric to frame at corners, using silk tacks or push pins. Stretch fabric taut; secure on all sides, staggering placement of tacks, so none are directly across from each other. If silk dyes require any preparation, follow manufacturer's directions.

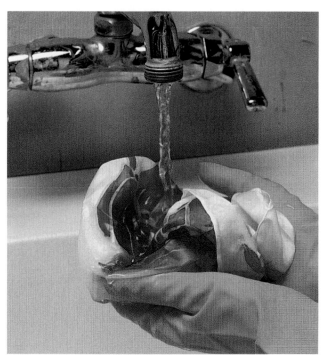

3 Apply dye, using brush or foam applicator. Follow tips for applying dye to silk, on page 63. Use separate brush or foam applicator for each dye color. Allow fabric to dry completely.

4 Remove fabric from frame. Heat-set dyes using steam method (opposite). Rinse fabric in cool water to remove resist; allow to dry. Press.

1 Sandwich dyed, dry fabric between two or three layers of unprinted newsprint. Roll paper and fabric together into a loose bundle; secure bundle with rubber band. Newsprint keeps the dyes from migrating to other parts of the fabric.

2 Pour 2 to 3 cups (500 to 750 mL) of water in a deep kettle. Place bundle on steaming net or raised rack, several inches above water. Shape a dome of aluminum foil; place over bundle.

3 Place a folded terry towel over kettle to absorb excess moisture; place lid on kettle. Heat water to boiling; steam bundle for 30 minutes, turning bundle over after 15 minutes. Steam must rise and penetrate fabric, without getting fabric wet.

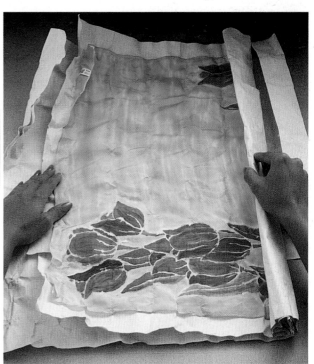

4 Remove from heat. Unwrap bundle immediately.

Applicator bottle method. Purchase metal-tip gutta applicator bottle for best results; it may be included with purchase of resist. Some have interchangeable tips for different line widths. Hold bottle vertically; press tip firmly against suspended fabric. Squeeze bottle and move along design lines at an even pace. Practice before applying resist to project.

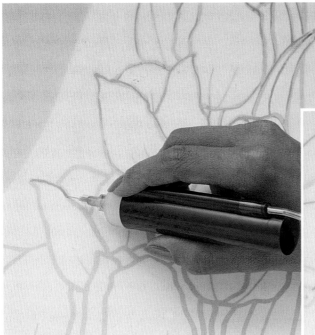

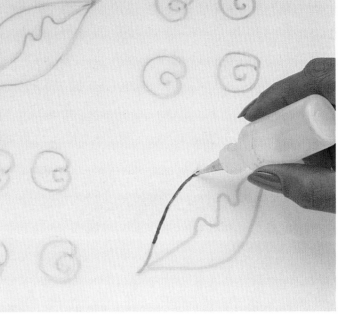

Airpen method. Read manufacturer's directions. Assemble tool using tip in size suitable for desired line width. Cover air hole with index finger to release resist from pen; move tip steadily along design lines. Practice until you feel comfortable with tool.

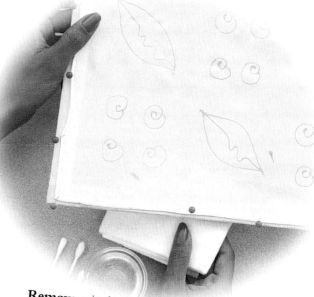

Hold fabric up to light and check from underside to see that resist has penetrated fabric completely and that there are no gaps in resist lines. Every design section must be completely enclosed.

Remove mistakes immediately with cool water. Press folded fabric to underside in mistake area; swab away resist from right side, using cotton-tipped swab.

Raise stretcher bars or hoop higher off surface as wet fabric sags to prevent it from touching work surface. Or, remove silk tacks or push pins one at a time, and restretch fabric.

Dip tip of paintbrush or foam applicator in dye; touch to center of desired area. Allow dye to transfer from brush to fabric and spread toward resist. Ease dye toward outer edges of area as necessary; using tip of brush. Do not use a typical stroking motion. Use separate brush or applicator for each color.

Highlighting. Apply water to wet dye in an area you wish to highlight, using small clean paintbrush. Or, drag wet brush through area. Rinse brush and repeat as necessary.

Blending. Apply two different colors in one area, and allow dyes to run together. Wet area with water before blending for more subtle blending. Apply dyes to dry fabric for more controlled effect.

Sun Printing

Harness a little solar power to create stunning shadow designs on fabric. Special sunlight-reactive Setacolor transparent paints by Pebeo are so easy to use, even children will find this process fun and exciting. You simply brush the diluted paint onto the fabric, position the object that will resist (there's that word again) the sun, place the fabric in the sunlight, and wait. If you can't wait for a sunny day, you can use a halogen lamp or a sun lamp that emits ultraviolet light.

Begin with fabric that is all white **(1)**, already dyed **(2),** or commercially printed **(3).** Almost any fabric will work, including cotton, polyester, cotton/polyester blend, silk, and linen. The finer the weave, the more distinct the shadow will appear. Dilute the Setacolor paint with water; two parts water to one part paint or up to eight parts water to one part paint. The more diluted the paint, the more transparent the color will be, and the more faint the shadow will appear.

MATERIALS

- ❏ Finely woven fabric, as described above.
- ❏ Hard, flat surface, such as plywood, foam core, or heavy cardboard.
- ❏ Setacolor paints; bowl for diluting paint; foam applicator.
- ❏ Objects for resisting the sun, such as leaves, feathers, wooden shapes, metal or plastic washers, lace, paper cutouts, anything with an interesting shape.
- ❏ Sunlight, or other suitable light source.

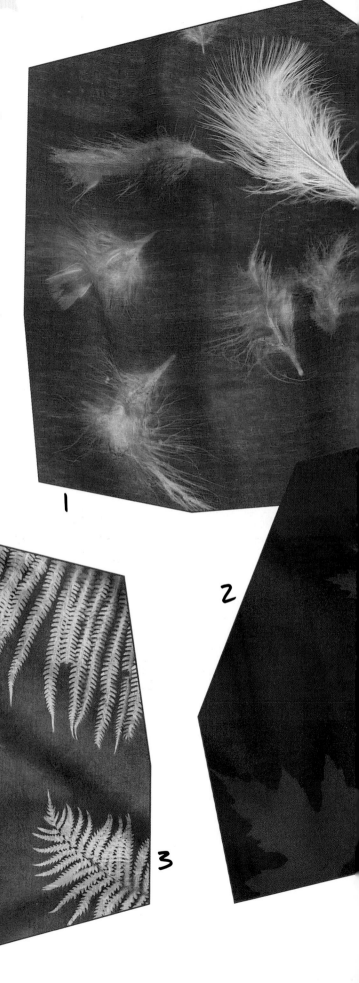

1

2

3

1 Stretch fabric taut over a smooth, waterproof, transportable surface; secure outer edges with tape or pins. Dilute desired colors of Setacolor transparent paint. Spread paint on fabric, using foam applicator; cover fabric entirely.

2 Place opaque objects (resists) on wet fabric. For best results, objects should lay flat on fabric. Move fabric to sunny, still spot. Allow fabric to dry completely.

3 Remove resists. Heat-set fabric by pressing it, facedown, at temperature appropriate for fabric. Or preheat oven to 210°F (99°C), then turn off oven. Place fabric on aluminum foil in oven for 10 minutes. Wash, dry, and press fabric.

Discharging Dye •••

Discharging is a fast and relatively easy method for creating designs by removing dye from colored or printed fabric. Bleach applied to the fabric begins to remove color immediately and continues to do so until the fabric is rinsed in cold water and neutralized. For best results, the bleach should be allowed to work no longer than ten minutes. After rinsing, the fabric must be immersed in a vinegar/water bath to neutralize the bleach. Because the bleach works fast, prepare the cold water bath before you apply the bleach. The rinsing and neutralizing can be done in buckets for small pieces of fabric, or in the washing machine for larger pieces.

Designs are created in the fabric by discharging the dye from certain areas while leaving the remainder of the fabric its original color. This can be done in several ways, depending on the desired results. For some methods, household bleach is simply diluted with water in a 50/50 solution and applied to the fabric with a foam brush, sprayed over the fabric surface, or squirted out of a syringe. For more control, use a thickened bleach, readily available in the form of household cleaning gels or dishwashing gel, such as Sunlight®, Comet®, or Clorox Cleanup®. To speed up results, add up to 50% more bleach to these gels. Apply the gel to the fabric, using a printing block (page 36), stencil (page 42), or screen (page 46). A mechanical resist (page 50) can be incorporated by pleating, folding, or twisting the fabric in any of the methods on page 56 before applying the bleach.

Select dark or brightly colored rayon or cotton fabrics for the most profound results. Bleach damages protein fibers like silk and wool. Prewash, dry, and press the fabric before discharging the dye. Work in a well-ventilated area, and wear rubber gloves and protective goggles. If you are spraying the bleach solution, the ideal conditions are to work outdoors with a breeze at your back. Cover the work surface with plastic and wear old clothes because you will inevitably get a stray drop of bleach where you don't want it.

Because the results are unpredictable and permanent, test each fabric before proceeding to determine what color or colors your fabric will become and how long to leave the bleach on the fabric to get the desired results. You may be surprised at the colors that are produced with the discharging process. Dark blue fabric, for instance, may turn various shades of pink or peach. If you enjoy the challenge of creating without guarantees or controlled results, discharging may be the method for you.

2 Watch discharging process carefully. When desired effect has been reached, gently transfer fabric into cold water bucket; rinse thoroughly. Or, transfer fabric into washing machine and turn on to run through wash cycle. Clean any tools, stencils, or screens thoroughly to remove all traces of bleach.

1 Cover padded work surface with plastic. Prepare bucket of cold water for rinsing. Prepare bucket of neutralizing solution, mixing 1 cup (250 mL) white vinegar in 1 gallon (3.8 L) water. Or, fill washing machine with cold water. Apply bleach solution or gel to fabric using one of the methods opposite.

3 Squeeze out excess water. Transfer fabric to neutralizing solution; allow to soak for ½ hour, agitating occasionally. Or, pour 1 cup (250 mL) white vinegar into washing machine as it begins rinse cycle. Squeeze or spin out excess solution. Hang or machine dry fabric.

Stenciling. Apply bleach solution or gel over stencil, using foam applicator, sponge, or synthetic stencil brush. Bleach solution works well for textured fabrics or pile fabrics, such as cotton velveteen. Bleach gel is recommended for smooth, tightly woven fabrics.

Stamping. Apply thin, even coat of bleach gel to stamp or other item, using foam applicator. Reapply gel after each print.

Work on 1 yard (0.95 m) or less of fabric to obtain multiple images with relatively equal results. Work in random pattern, rather than progressing from one end of fabric to the other; designs applied first will have more profound results than those applied last.

Place desired items over fabric surface to create mechanical resist (page 50). Spray fabric with bleach solution, using household spray bottle. Wear protective clothing, goggles, and mask.

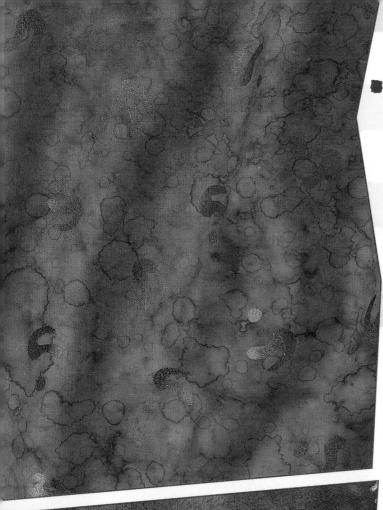

Metallic foil designs offer a crowning touch when layered over the top of artistically dyed or painted fabric. Foil has a smooth glimmering quality, different from the subtle glint of metallic paint. Aside from their glimmering richness, foiled designs also add a visual depth and contrast that catches your eye and invites you to look closer.

Foiling is a relatively easy technique and, once applied, the foiled fabric can be laundered with no adverse effects. However, dry cleaning should be avoided. An adhesive is first applied to the fabric in the desired area. When ironed facedown onto the fabric, the metallic foil adheres to the adhesive pattern. Adhesives include washable, flexible fabric glues, such as Stitchless® and Jewel Glue™ by Delta Technical Coatings and Plexi® Glue by Jones Tones™. In another method, fusible web, such as Pellon® Wonder-Under™, cut into shapes, is used to bond the foil to the fabric. Suitable foils must be intended for use on fabric. See the source list on page 112.

Glue can be applied to the fabric in different ways, depending on the desired result. For the clearest, most consistent design, apply the glue by screen printing (page 46). Other suitable methods include stamping (page 36), brushing it on with a foam applicator, applying it through a squeeze bottle, or pouncing with a damp sea sponge.

Materials

❑ Adhesive in the form of glue (suitable brands listed above), or fusible web.

❑ Tools as desired, for applying glue.

❑ Foil intended for use on fabric.

❑ Iron; press cloth.

1 Glue method. Apply glue to fabric, using desired tools and techniques. Wash tools immediately. Allow glue to dry.

Fusible web method. Trace desired shapes on paper backing of fusible web; cut out. Fuse shapes to fabric, following manufacturer's directions. Remove paper backing.

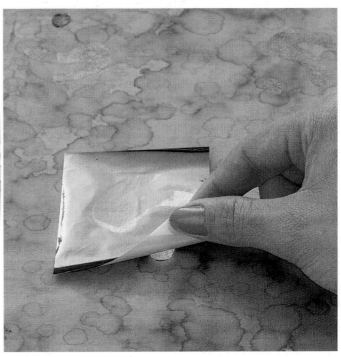

2 Place foil, colored side up, over fabric; cover with press cloth. Press with iron set at high heat for 10 seconds in each spot. Allow to cool. Peel cellophane from foil. Repeat as necessary to foil all areas.

Photo Transfer

If you have access to an inkjet printer or color copier, either at home or at the local copy shop, you can transfer photographic images to fabric for artistic applications. Actually, any image you can copy, scan, or create on your computer screen can be transferred to fabric with this method. With computer technology, scissors, and a creative mind, the application possibilities are endless. The memory craze is translated by quilters into heirloom quilts that depict photographic family history. Cloth dolls may carry photographic faces of real people. A cherished photo can be heat-set into the fabric cover of an album or diary. Memorable mountain views might adorn a favorite hiking jacket.

Basically, the photographic image is copied onto special transfer paper and then heat-set onto the fabric. This is done in one of two methods, using either a color laser copier or a color inkjet printer. You can access a color laser copier at most copy shops, where the image is simply copied onto the transfer paper. Check with the copy shop to see if you must furnish your own transfer paper and the specific kind of paper their copier requires. To use an inkjet printer, the photograph is first scanned into the computer and then printed out on transfer paper. Transfer papers are specifically designed for one method or the other; color laser copiers have a heating element, whereas inkjet printers do not. The papers are not interchangeable, so be sure to check the label carefully.

Read and follow the paper manufacturer's directions for transferring the image; the directions on page 74 are very general. Be sure to reverse or "mirror" the image before printing so that it will transfer to the fabric in the original direction. Use a dry iron heated to the highest setting or a heat press set between 350°F (180°C) and 375°F (190°C) for the transfer process. Another difference among the transfer papers is that some must be peeled away while they are still hot. Others are peeled away after they have cooled. Removing hot-peel paper takes a little dexterity, since the paper backing has to remain hot in order to peel off without damaging the image. The cool-peel papers are easier on your fingers and easier to use. With either paper, try to remove the backing with one continuous motion, peeling in the direction of the fabric grain in order to avoid distortion or unwanted lines in the image.

Transfer photographic images to white fabric for the truest color. Because the transfer is transparent, any color or design in the fabric will affect the image. Fine cotton with a high thread count produces the sharpest image; looser weaves and textures distort the image. However, you may want to experiment with pastels, tiny pale prints, or slight texture if an altered image is part of your creative intention!

Materials

❑ Photograph, black and white or color.
❑ Photo transfer paper appropriate for method used.
❑ Color laser copier or computer, scanner, and color inkjet printer.
❑ Iron or heat press.
❑ White finely woven cotton fabric, or fabric of choice.

1 Print photograph or image on transfer paper, using color laser copier; reverse image before printing, so that image will appear normal when transferred to fabric. Or, scan photo, reverse image, and print on transfer paper, using color inkjet printer.

2 Cut away any excess transfer paper or unwanted portions of image. Place fabric, right side up, on firm, lightly padded surface. Place transfer paper, image side down, over fabric. Heat iron to highest setting; do not use steam.

3 Heat fabric with iron; place transfer facedown on fabric, and smooth onto fabric with fingers. Place iron on back of transfer; press down as hard as you can. Hold in one area for up to 30 seconds before moving to another area. Repeat until entire transfer has been pressed; shift angle of iron often to avoid steam vent marks.

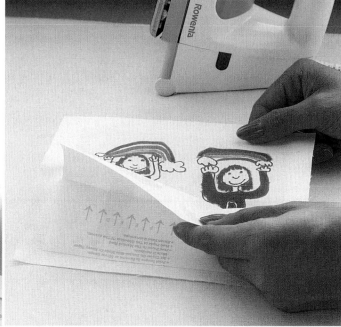

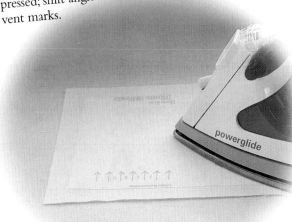

4 Press again over entire transfer sheet. For hot-peel paper, lift one corner slightly to check transfer. Immediately peel paper backing in one continuous motion, peeling in the direction of the fabric grain. Allow to cool. For cool-peel paper, allow paper to cool completely before checking transfer and peeling.

Enlarge or reduce photo size as desired before printing. Check to see that increase in size does not distort or blur image by printing on plain paper first.

Economize by scanning or copying several photos at one time. Cut individual images apart after printing onto transfer paper.

Copy several photos onto plain paper. Create an interesting collage by cutting them apart, trimming away unwanted areas, and overlapping images. Then copy collage onto transfer paper.

Print black and white photos in sepia tones for a nostalgic touch, using either the color laser copier or the inkjet printer. Print out the image on plain paper to test first. Or, print a black and white photo on transfer paper, and transfer it to a pastel fabric.

stitched
designs

With needle and thread as your paintbrush,
translate your creative ideas into colorful
designs, rich in texture and full of surprise.
Imagine the possibilities!

oolong

darjeeling

Ginseng

Free-motion Embroidery • • • •

Your sewing machine may be your most valuable and versatile tool for interpreting your inspirations into works of art. Far beyond the utilitarian uses of sewing seams and altering hems, even a basic sewing machine with straight-stitch and zigzag capabilities has the capacity for creating fascinating thread "sketches" and machine embroidered "paintings."

While painted and dyed images offer color, design, and visual depth, machine embroidery goes one step farther, adding wonderful tactile surface texture. With the creative use of thread color, stitch placement, and stitch density, you can stitch outlined sketches, rhythmic flowing lines, or filled-in and shaded images. Free-motion embroidery can accent or repeat the lines of a stamped, stenciled, or screen-printed design. For some appliqué techniques, machine embroidery is both a functional and decorative element of the overall design.

If you can draw or paint, you can learn to use your sewing machine to stitch free-flowing images and designs on fabric. The basic difference is that instead of moving a pencil or paintbrush across a stationary surface, you are moving the surface around under a stationary needle. Even if you think you can't draw or paint, you can undoubtedly trace over a line, in which case you can transfer your design to the fabric first. Like any other skill, once you learn these basic free-motion stitching techniques, the more you practice the better you'll get.

For free-motion machine embroidery, the feed dogs are either covered or lowered, if possible; the stitch length and direction are controlled by the artist. There is usually no need for a presser foot, though a darning foot can be used. Sketching and outlining are usually done with the machine set for a straight stitch. A zigzag stitch can be used for filling in and shading areas. To prevent puckering and help you establish a smooth, flowing motion, you must temporarily stabilize the fabric in some way. Most often, the fabric is held taut in an embroidery hoop. Tear-away stabilizer is used on the wrong side of the fabric for extra stability. Water-soluble stabilizer, used either on the right or wrong side, is useful for fabrics that are washable.

Machine embroidery threads, in cotton, rayon, and metallics, come in a wide array of colors. They vary in weight, from 30-weight to 60-weight, with the lower numbers being the heavier threads. Select needle type and size according to the fabric as well as the thread. Needle sizes 70/9 and 80/11 are suitable for cotton embroidery thread; for rayon and metallic threads, use size 80/11 or 90/14. Fine cotton thread is used in the bobbin, unless the fabric is meant to be decorative on both sides, in which case the same embroidery thread is wound on the bobbin. Run a test sample, and adjust the stitch tension, if necessary.

Keep fabric taut in a ¼" (6 mm) thick embroidery hoop, in a diameter that is easy to work with under the presser foot. Wrap inner ring of wooden hoop with cotton twill tape to protect delicate fabrics.

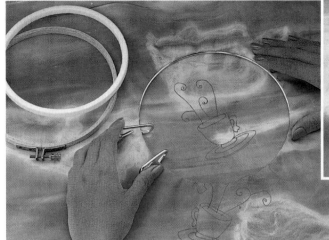

Place fabric, right side up, over outer ring; push inner ring in place, keeping fabric taut and grainline undistorted. Push inner ring through to underside about ⅛" (3 mm).

Sit directly in front of the machine needle, with hands resting comfortably on sides of hoop; do not grip hoop. Guide fabric with wrist motions, resting elbows on table or on books stacked around bed of machine, so shoulders are not tense.

Move the fabric at a smooth, even pace while running machine at moderate to fast speed to obtain short even stitches. Develop skill by writing words; practice loops, circles, or stipple patterns.

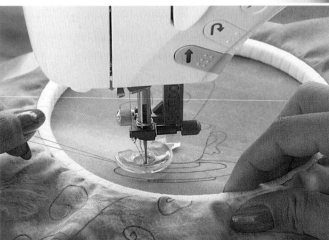

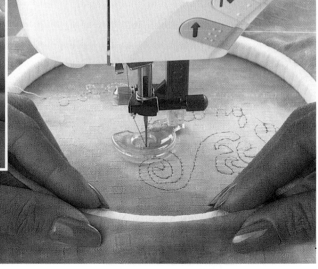

Lower presser foot lever, engaging tension discs. This is easy to overlook when sewing without a presser foot or with a darning foot. Bring bobbin thread through to right side, and hold both threads to one side as you begin stitching. Stitch in place a few times to secure stitches at beginning and end or whenever changing colors.

Fill in areas using wide zigzag stitch; move fabric side to side, stitching rows directly next to each other. To blend one color into another, leave irregular border; stitch into border at varying depths with adjoining color.

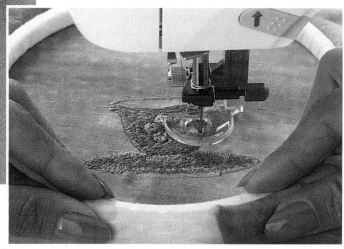

Adjust tension so that top thread is pulled slightly to underside for fabric with definite "right side." Adjust tension so that stitches look nearly the same from both sides for a reversible look.

Outline areas with two or three tightly spaced rows of straight stitches. Use the same technique to add design lines to filled-in areas.

Use quilter's gloves or rubber fingertips instead of a hoop when minimal stabilizing is required or when you want to stitch freely over wide spans of fabric without breaking the stitching line.

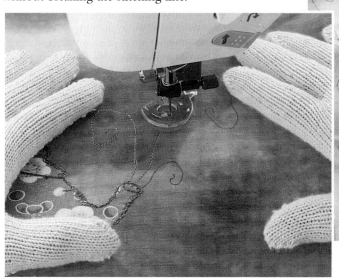

Mark design on water-soluble stabilizer, and pin it to fabric surface, if desired.

···APPLIQUÉ

Many fabric artists incorporate some form of appliqué into their creations, thus adding color and design with the bonus of textural interest. In simple terms, an appliqué is a fabric cutout attached to the surface of a larger piece of fabric. However, a fabric cutout can be interpreted in countless ways, from a single shape to a complex puzzle of interacting shapes. An appliqué can be a photographic image transferred to fabric or a stenciled design that is lined and beaded. It may not even be fabric at all, but rather a unique found object that is incorporated into the surface design of the fabric.

Equally as endless are the possible methods for attaching that appliqué to the surface. Satin-stitched appliqué is certainly a viable option, and one that is often appropriate. However, there are many other methods of application that are effective and appropriate in the right circumstances. The key is to attach the appliqué in a way that is consistent with the form and function of the item being created while complementing both the appliqué and the surrounding fabric.

These examples and brief descriptions give you a glimpse at the possibilities. Some methods are taught in more detail on the pages that follow.

Forms of Appliqué

1 **Raw-edge appliqué** (page 84). Edges of the cutout are not finished or turned under. The cutout may be secured with straight stitches, multistitch-zigzag, or free-motion stitching. Because the edges are not emphasized, the cutout seems to merge with the background fabric.

2 **Satin-stitched appliqué**. Tightly spaced zigzag stitches form a small ridge around the cutout, accenting the edges and giving the appliqué prominence.

3 **Couched appliqué**. Cutouts are secured by couching a decorative cord around the outer edge, creating a ridge and finishing the cut edges.

4 **Lined appliqué** (page 88). Each cutout is lined to the edge. Pieces can be applied to lie flat on the surface or secured with internal stitches that allow the edges to rise, revealing the lining and creating a three-dimensional effect.

5 **Negative appliqué** (page 91). Background fabric is cut away in desired shapes to reveal contrasting fabric layered underneath. Cut edges can be treated in a variety of ways to make the appliqué blend into the background fabric or create depth or dimension.

6 **Bias strip appliqué** (page 95). Tubes or strips of fabric are secured to a background fabric, creating raised designs. Knots, beads, or other interesting objects may be incorporated.

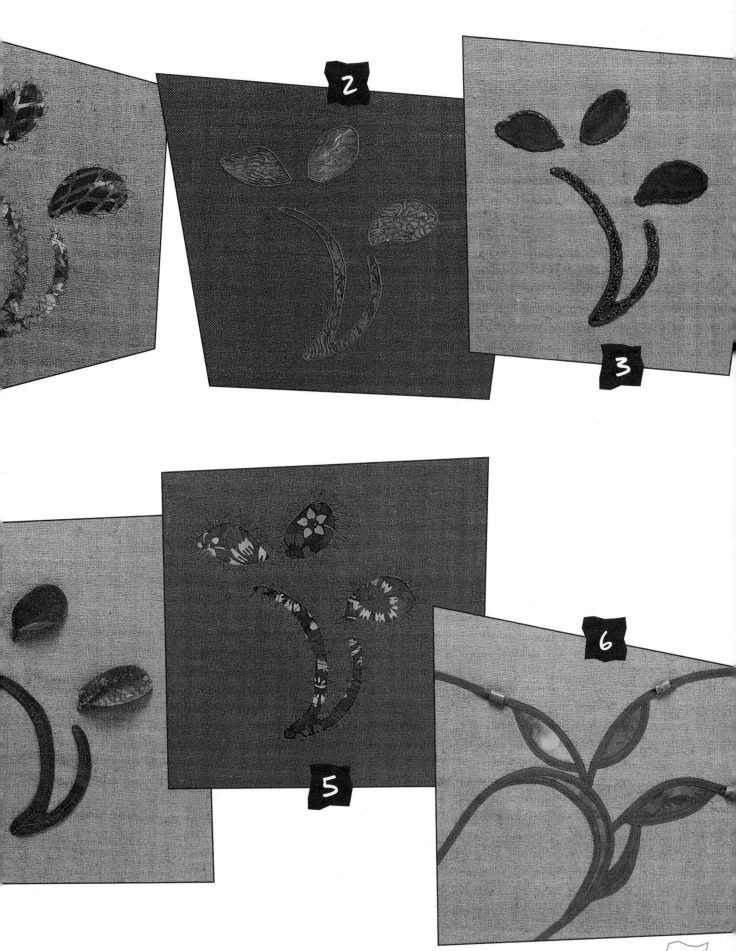

Raw-edge Appliqué

There are many styles of raw-edge appliqué, most of them conforming to a few basic principles. Shapes are usually cut free-hand, though an artist may get inspiration from a printed design and may even draw shapes onto the fabric before cutting. In some styles, motifs are cut from printed fabric and applied as appliqués to another background fabric. Fabrics are usually firm and closely woven because the cut edges are neither finished nor turned under. Appliqué edges will fray slightly in wearing and laundering, softening the design edges. Nonwoven fabrics provide clean edges that will not fray and require little sewing. Almost anything, including nets, laces, fringed selvages, and scraps of needlework may be used to achieve certain design effects.

Hold motifs in place temporarily with pins or with wash-away adhesive spray. Then secure the appliqué with a machine-guided straight stitch or multistitch-zigzag, changing stitch length and width to create interest. Use free-motion thread sketching for a very effective method of attachment. Choose thread color to match the fabric for inconspicuous stitching. Add or amplify design details by using contrasting colors and shades of thread. Select a bobbin thread to match the background fabric, and adjust the tension, if necessary, to prevent the bobbin thread from coming to the surface. Launder the fabric after applying the appliqué to gently fray the edges and give the entire appliqué a softer appearance.

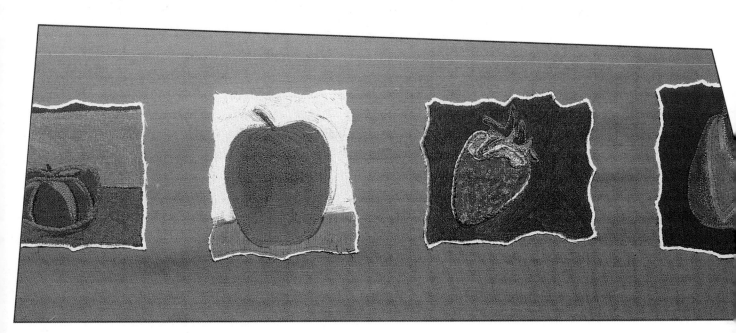

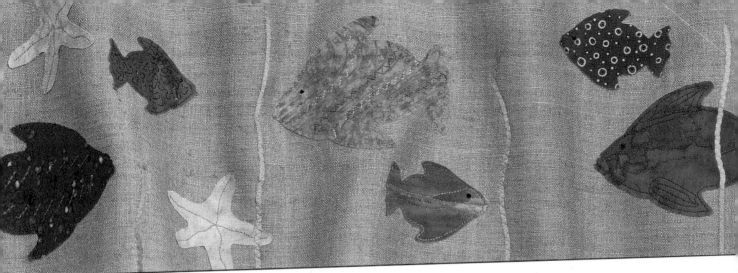

Individual Motifs

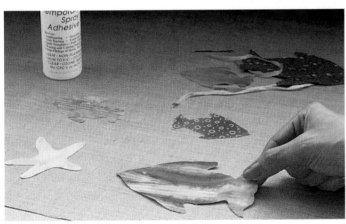

1 Cut shapes from selected fabrics. Arrange on the background fabric; secure temporarily to the background fabric using adhesive spray, pins, or glue stick.

2 Stitch to background fabric, using machine-guided or free-motion edgestitching for a flat design. Secure with interior stitches along design lines for a more dimensional effect. Stitch interior design lines, as desired.

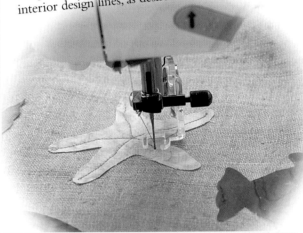

Print Motif Appliqué

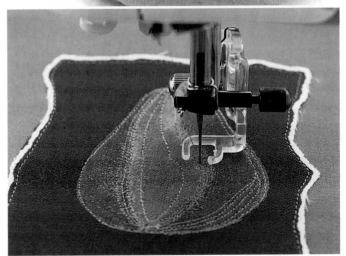

1 Cut motifs from printed fabric and reposition them on the background fabric in a new arrangement. For instance, create a border print with motifs cut from an all-over print fabric. Secure temporarily.

2 Secure with free-motion stitching ⅛" (3 mm) from cut edges. Stitch free-motion thread sketching (page 79) to interiors of motifs to soften and blend colors and emphasize design details. For textural interest, couch decorative cords or yarns over strong design lines.

Abstract Appliqué

2 Add patches of color, one at a time, overlapping as necessary to build design. Stitch appropriate pattern in each patch.

1 Plan your design, drawing inspiration from a photograph or painting, perhaps. Cut amorphous patches of various sizes from solid colors or muted prints to roughly represent elements of the design. Position patch for most recessed element of design on background fabric; secure temporarily. Stitch over patch, using free-motion technique in a pattern that resembles the element you want to convey. For instance, circles over a blue patch suggest a clump of grapes. Trim edges.

•• Fabric Collage ••

1 Working from a photograph or painting, select a multitude of fabrics with small patterns in different colors and values to achieve a painterly effect. Convert the photograph to a line drawing; cut shapes to represent all the divisions in the drawing.

2 Layer pieces on background fabric to fill in the design; secure temporarily. Secure pieces, using free-motion stitching, or multistitch-zigzag.

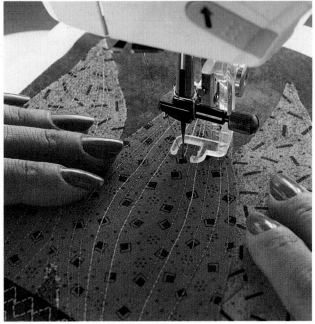

3 Add shading and accent design lines with free-motion thread sketching, satin stitching, or couched yarns.

Lined Appliqué

Lined appliqués are completely finished around the outer edge before they are attached to the background fabric. Any fabric is a candidate for the appliqué fabric, as long as its character and color provide the desired effect. Delicate or loosely woven fabrics can be stabilized with lightweight fusible knit interfacing, giving them added body and minimizing fraying around the closely trimmed edges.

Suitable lining fabric varies, depending on the method of attachment. The appliqué can be attached by invisibly blind-stitching around the outer edge. Using this method, the lining is entirely hidden, and therefore any sheer or lightweight tightly woven fabric is suitable. Tulle netting works well because it does not ravel and it allows you the extra advantage of being able to see through the lining when positioning it on the fabric. Tulle lining also enables you to use sheer fabric or lace for the appliqué, opening up a new realm of possibilities.

Another method of attachment utilizes stitched design lines on the interior of the appliqué. With this method, the outer edge of the appliqué rises from the surface, creating more dimension and exposing the lining to some degree. A sculpted effect can be created by manipulating the appliqué into a raised and shaped form before securing it with internal stitches. For these techniques, you may want to select either self fabric or a coordinating lightweight fabric for the lining, incorporating it into your overall design.

How to Sew a Lined Appliqué

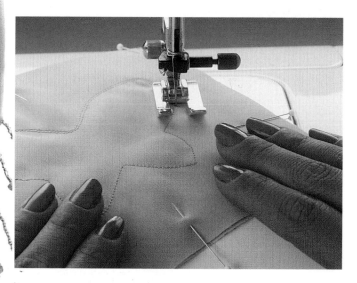

1 Trace desired shape onto wrong side of lining fabric. Place lining fabric over appliqué fabric, right sides together; pin. Stitch all around design, using short stitches. Stitch again just outside first row of stitches.

2 Trim close to second stitching line. Cut small slit in lining, away from outer edge. If appliqué is dimensional, slit lining in area that will not be exposed.

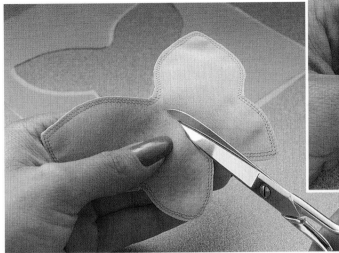

3 Turn appliqué right side out through slit. Push out any curves or points, using narrow, blunt tool, such as a cuticle stick; press.

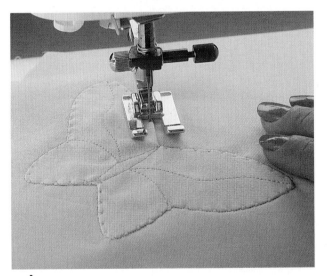

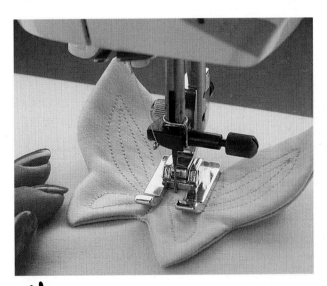

4 **Blindstitch method.** Stitch any internal design lines. Pin appliqué to background fabric. Thread machine with invisible nylon thread; blindstitch on background fabric as close to appliqué as possible, just catching appliqué edge with left-hand swing of needle.

4 **Dimensional method.** Stitch any internal design lines not intended to secure appliqué. Secure appliqué to background fabric along remaining internal design lines, hiding slit in lining.

4 **Sculpted method.** Stitch any internal design lines not intended to secure appliqué. Manipulate appliqué as desired; secure to background fabric with additional stitching on internal design lines.

Negative Appliqué 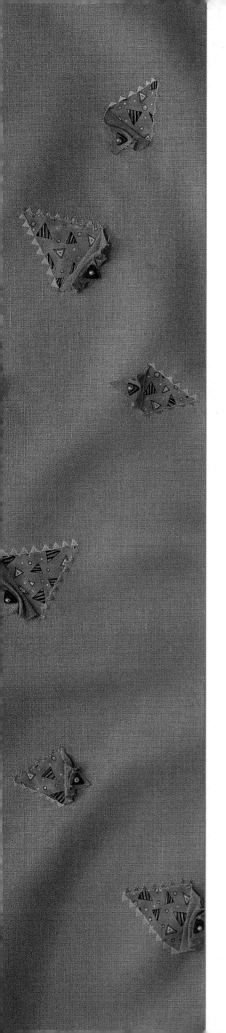••••

Unlike other methods in which appliqués are sewn on top of the surface fabric, negative appliqué methods involve the removal of surface fabric to reveal appliqué fabric layered underneath. The technique may be as simple as cutting openings in the top fabric and treating the cut edges in a manner similar to raw-edge appliqué (page 84). In another technique, called shuttered windows, geometric openings are partially cut in the surface fabric, and excess fabric flaps are secured to one side. This method adds dimension to the surface and offers tantalizing peeks into the fabric beneath it. Faced openings have a finished edge all around the opening, providing a dramatic framework for showcasing interesting printed designs or photo transfers (page 72) perhaps. To further enhance the appliqué, a contrasting facing is rolled slightly to the right side, resembling the matting in framed artwork.

▮ ▮ How to Sew Raw-edge Negative Appliqués ▮ ▮

I Cut openings in surface fabric; discard cutouts. Spray wrong side of surface fabric with temporary fabric adhesive. Place appliqué fabrics face-down over openings on wrong side of surface fabric.

2 Stitch over openings from right side, using desired stitching techniques such as free-motion stippling or thread sketching or machine-guided decorative stitches.

2 Cut all but one side of opening, leaving fabric flap; pin flap to side of shape. Stitch over previous stitches, using satin stitches or embroidery pattern.

1 Mark desired straight-edged geometric openings on surface fabric. Cut on one side. Layer over appliqué fabric; stitch around each marked opening, using short straight stitches just outside marked lines.

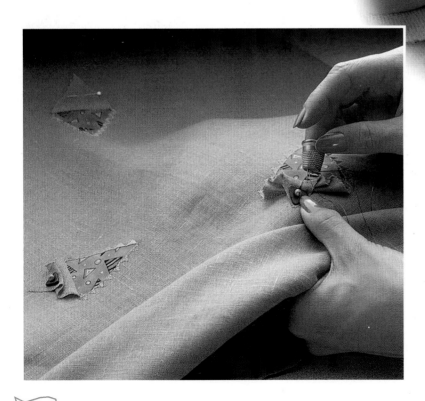

3 Roll, pleat, or gather flap back away from opening. Tack in place or secure with hand-stitched bead.

1 Cut facing fabric at least 1" (2.5 cm) larger than intended opening. Cut appliqué of same size. Draw opening on wrong side of facing; place over surface fabric in desired location, right sides together. Stitch around marked opening, using short straight stitches. Stitch again within opening, next to first stitches.

2 Trim away facing and surface fabric ⅛" (3 mm) inside inner stitched line; clip curves and into corners up to stitches.

3 Turn facing to inside; press, rolling facing slightly to right side, if desired. Turn surface fabric over. Pin appliqué to facing, right sides together. Stitch ¼" (6 mm) from edges, keeping surface fabric out of the way.

4 Embellish appliqué, if desired. On right side of surface fabric, stitch around outside of opening through all layers, using decorative stitch or free-motion stitching.

Bias Strip Appliqué •••••••

Quilters commonly use bias tape or tubes to create quilts with stained glass or Celtic designs. The same techniques can easily be used to embellish fabric for clothing or home decorating projects. Prefolded fusible bias tape, available in several colors and metallics, makes quick work of intricate designs. Cut and sew bias tube appliqués from other fabrics, using convenient tools, such as the Fasturn®, for turning tubes right side out, and flat aluminum or nylon press bars, if flat strips with pressed folds are desired.

Depending on the look you want, select one of several methods for sewing the appliqué to the background fabric. Straight-stitch along the outer edges or sew decorative stitches down the center of flattened appliqué strips. For a raised effect, make tubes from fabric with more body, such as wool

crepe, and attach them with invisible machine or hand stitches. Shape them into tight curves, entwine or braid them into intricate designs, tie knots, or add beads for more dimension.

To determine the bias length needed for intricate designs, draw the design to size on paper. Tape the end of a string to a starting point in the design; trail the string over the design, following the lines until the entire pattern is complete. Then measure the total length of string used. Allow extra length for any knots and for maneuvering the tube to hide seams. Bias strips up to 65" (165.5 cm) long can be cut from the true bias of 45" (115 cm) fabric. For large complex designs, it may be easier to work with shorter lengths, hiding cut ends under intersections in the design.

■ ■ ■ ■ ■ ■ ■ How to Apply a Fusible Bias Tape Design ■ ■ ■ ■ ■ ■ ■

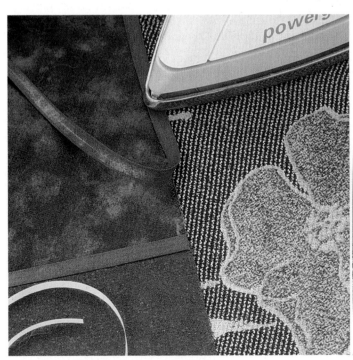

2 Edgestitch along both edges of tape. Or stitch down center of tape, using multistitch-zigzag or decorative machine stitch.

1 Mark design on right side of fabric. Stabilize background fabric, using desired method. Remove protective backing and fuse bias tape over design lines, working in small sections.

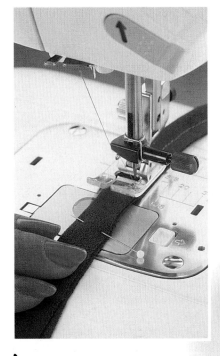

2 Turn tube right side out, using Fasturn or another suitable tool. For flattened tube, insert press bar into tube to manipulate tube into consistent width; press, keeping seam on back of tube. Move bar through tube until entire tube is pressed.

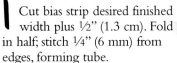

1 Cut bias strip desired finished width plus ½" (1.3 cm). Fold in half; stitch ¼" (6 mm) from edges, forming tube.

3 Mark design and stabilize background fabric. Arrange tube on design lines, securing as necessary with fabric glue or pins. Knot tube or add beads in desired positions.

4 Place fabric facedown over a light box. Secure tube, stitching by hand from wrong side, along center of tube.

Machine-stitched method. Blindstitch along one or both sides of tube, using invisible nylon thread. If tube crosses *under* itself, jump intersection; secure threads by stitching in place for several stitches before and after intersection. If tube crosses *over* itself, continue blind-stitching through intersection. Leave short lengths of tube unstitched before and after knots and beads.

Cover end with another appliqué.

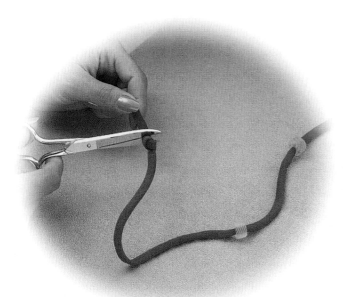

Turn under tape end before stitching. Turn in ends of tube; hand-stitch closed.

Knot tube end; trim close. Allow several inches (centimeters) to hang free from background fabric, if desired.

Plan appliqué ends to be caught in seams of project.

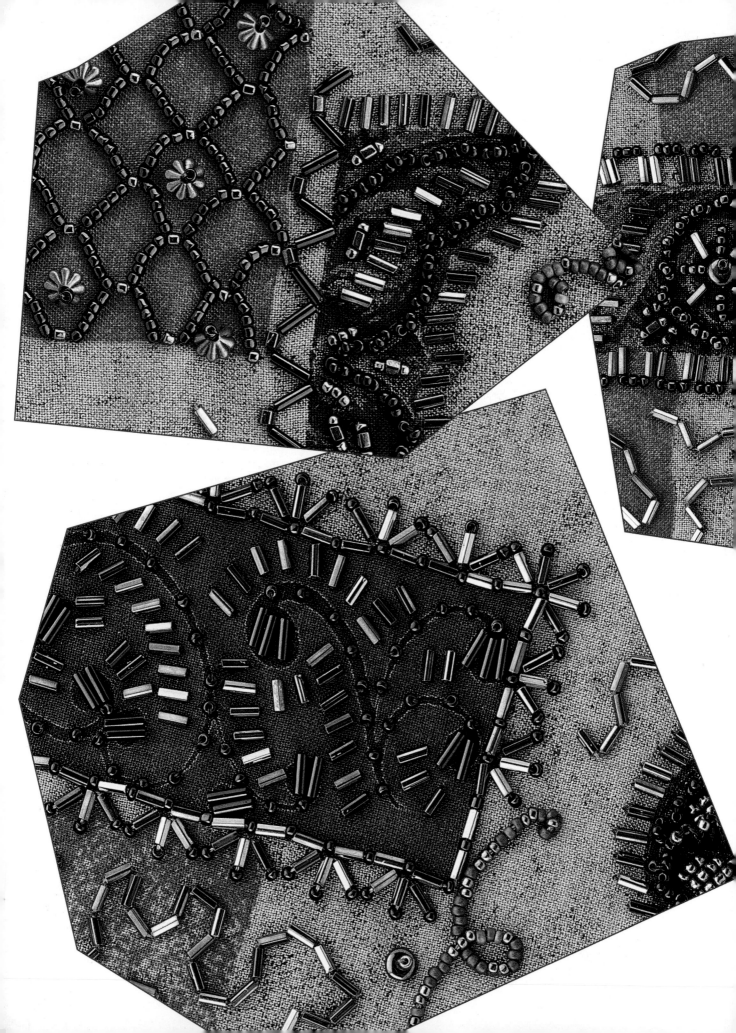

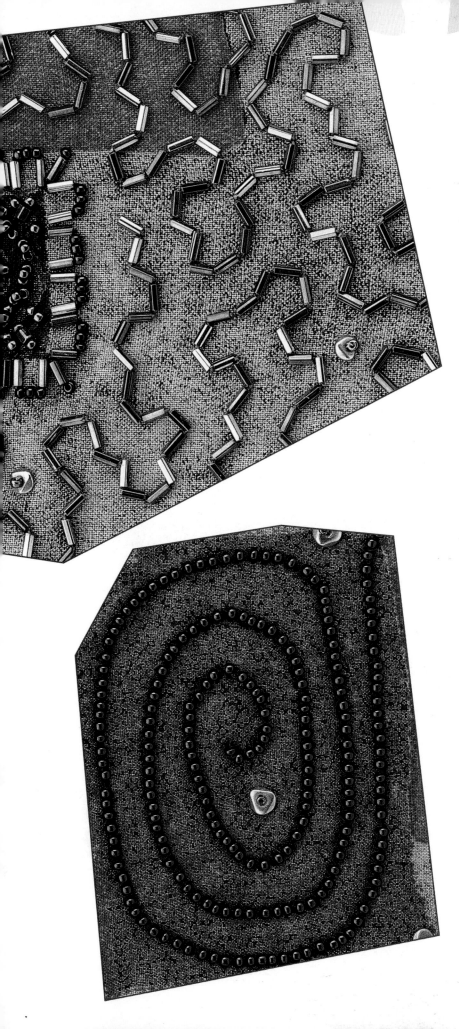

Beadwork on Fabric

Beadwork punctuates the surface of a fabric with texture and dazzling color. A heavily beaded design creates a focal point on a garment or quilt, while beads dispersed broadly over the fabric surface serve as a subtle accent. Beaded patterns may follow a transferred design of your choice or be incorporated into the fabric print.

Both machine sewing and hand stitching techniques are used for beadwork. Machine sewing is used to couch strung beads onto fabric for outlining, edging, or free-form lines. Loose beads are hand-sewn to fabric individually, in clusters or rows, or using specialty stitches to create intriguing dimensional effects. It is also possible to machine-stitch individual beads with holes large enough to accommodate the machine needle. This makes it possible to incorporate beads into free-motion machine embroidery. With experimentation, the possibilities are limitless. Even the basic stitches shown here can be used to produce a wide range of beaded effects.

Heavily beaded fabric will probably shrink in the beading process, so finish the bead-work before cutting out pieces for the project. Delay beading close to seamlines until the project is complete, allowing room for the presser foot to sew seams. Avoid beading in areas of high friction, such as under the arms on a garment.

The safest way to clean beaded fabric is to wash by hand and lay flat to dry. The clothes dryer inevitably chips, breaks, or melts beads. Dry-cleaning solvents can discolor or destroy some beads. Make a small sample with the beads and thread you intend to use in the project, and wash or dry-clean it, checking the beads for colorfastness and durability.

Beads are a choking hazard for small children, who are attracted to shiny colored objects. If children will be near your work area, be sure to put away beads when you are done working. Do not apply beads to clothing or accessories used by children.

Identifying Beads

Beads can be made of almost any material, including glass, plastic, polymer clay, shell, bone, wood, ceramic, metal, precious and semiprecious stone, and paper. The appropriateness of the beads for any project depends not only on their size, shape, and color, but also their weight and cleaning methods. For instance, while glass beads are the most common, they also are much heavier than plastic, paper, or wood, which is something to consider for a heavily beaded garment.

Beads are categorized according to their shape. Seed beads **(1)** are small and round, with a center hole. They are sold loose or on cotton strings, intended to be sewn separately or transferred to stronger beading thread for couching onto fabric. Bugle beads **(2)** are tubular, ranging in length from 2 to 4 mm. Drops **(3)** are pear-shaped, with a hole at the narrow end or lengthwise through the bead. Faceted beads **(4),** often transparent, have flat surfaces that are cut or molded. Roundels **(5)** are flat, doughnut-shaped beads. Fancy beads **(6)** of various shapes, sizes, materials, and hole placements have a wide range of decorative uses. Strung beads, for couching onto fabric, include rhinestones **(7),** molded plastic pearls **(8),** and cross-locked glass beads **(9).** The methods used for stringing them vary, but all are intended to keep the beads from coming apart when the string is cut.

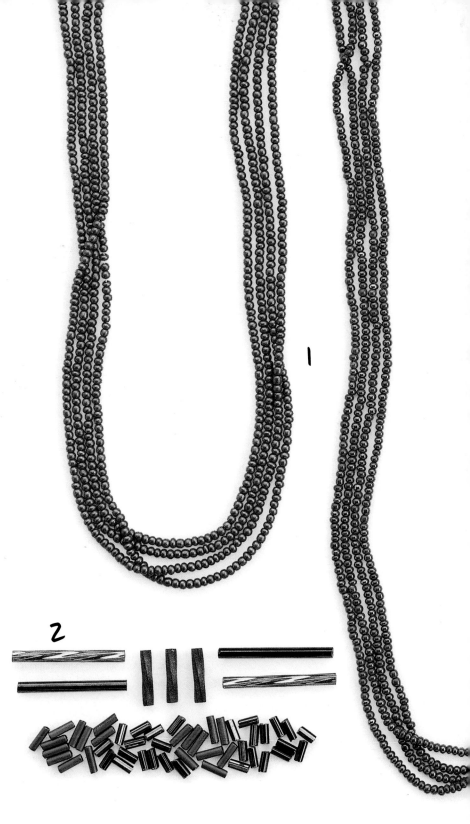

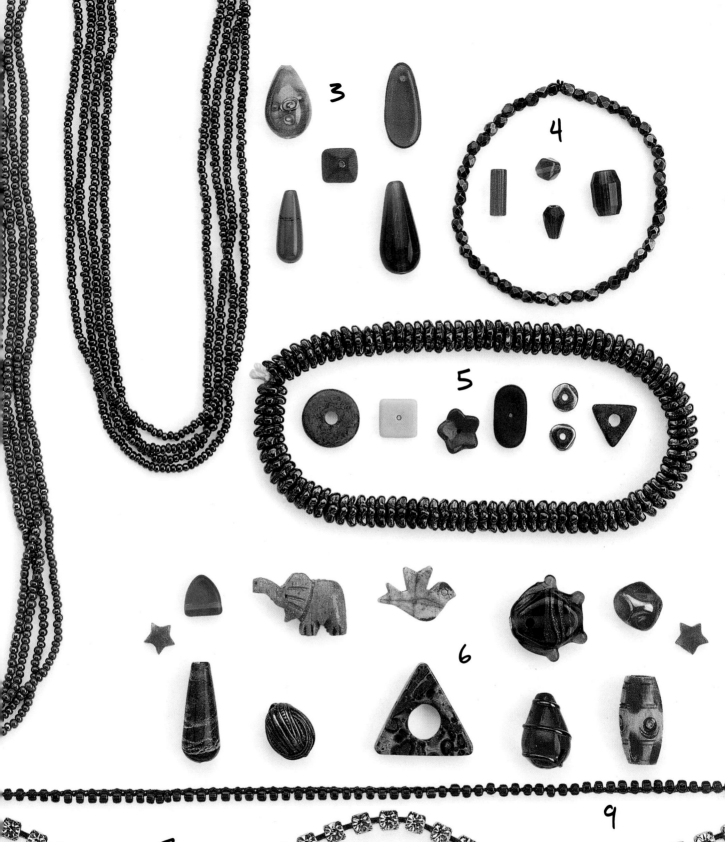

Beading Supplies

Beading needles **(1),** thinner and more flexible than standard hand-sewing needles, are available in sizes 10 to 14; the larger the number, the smaller the needle. They are usually sold in packs of twenty-five, a convenience due to their fragile nature.

Prewaxed twisted nylon beading thread **(2)** works well for most hand-sewn projects. A double strand of waxed cotton-wrapped polyester thread **(3)** is also recommended. Match the thread to the fabric, if you are using multiple colors of opaque beads. Transparent or semitransparent beads will be affected by the thread color. For machine sewing, use thread appropriate for the fabric and the technique. For instance, when beading is worked into free-motion embroidery, use cotton, rayon, or metallic embroidery thread **(4).** Use invisible nylon thread **(5)** for couching strung beads.

Beading bobbins **(6),** most commonly in sizes B and D, are wound with fine waxed nylon cord. They are used for hand sewing or for stringing beads before couching onto fabric, and are not intended to be inserted into the bobbin case of your sewing machine. The cord sticks to itself, unwinding as it is needed.

Liquid fray preventer **(7)** is useful for sealing knots on the underside of the fabric. Clear nail polish may also be used, but will leave a mark if it touches the fabric.

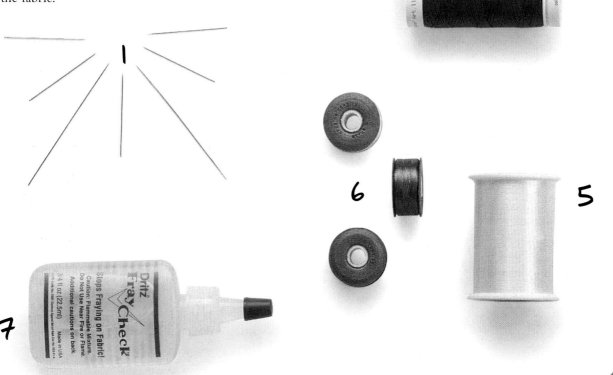

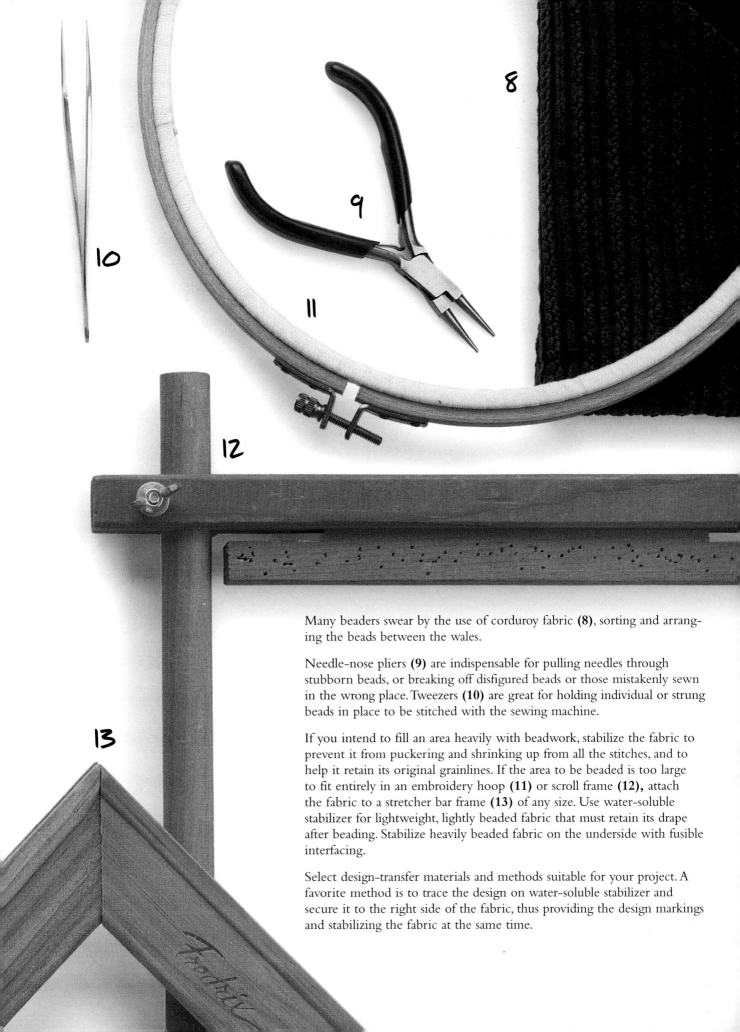

Many beaders swear by the use of corduroy fabric **(8)**, sorting and arranging the beads between the wales.

Needle-nose pliers **(9)** are indispensable for pulling needles through stubborn beads, or breaking off disfigured beads or those mistakenly sewn in the wrong place. Tweezers **(10)** are great for holding individual or strung beads in place to be stitched with the sewing machine.

If you intend to fill an area heavily with beadwork, stabilize the fabric to prevent it from puckering and shrinking up from all the stitches, and to help it retain its original grainlines. If the area to be beaded is too large to fit entirely in an embroidery hoop **(11)** or scroll frame **(12),** attach the fabric to a stretcher bar frame **(13)** of any size. Use water-soluble stabilizer for lightweight, lightly beaded fabric that must retain its drape after beading. Stabilize heavily beaded fabric on the underside with fusible interfacing.

Select design-transfer materials and methods suitable for your project. A favorite method is to trace the design on water-soluble stabilizer and secure it to the right side of the fabric, thus providing the design markings and stabilizing the fabric at the same time.

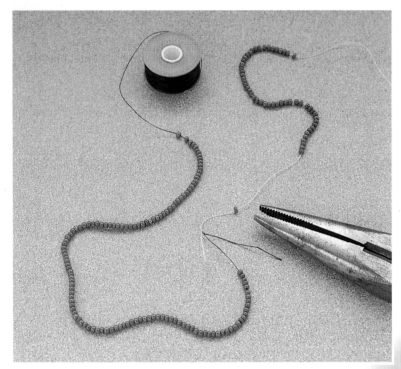

Attach beading foot or piping foot to conventional machine to sew over strung beads. The grooved bottom must be deep enough to allow presser foot to ride over beads without rubbing. Adjust zigzag length so one complete zigzag stitch is equal to distance between beads. Adjust stitch width so needle stitches over beads without hitting them.

Transfer beads from weak cotton thread onto beading bobbin before stitching to fabric. Knot threads together; slide beads from cotton thread onto bobbin thread. Break off any beads that will not slide over knot, using needle-nose pliers. Cut off cotton thread at knot; do not cut bobbin thread. Bobbin will unwind as needed.

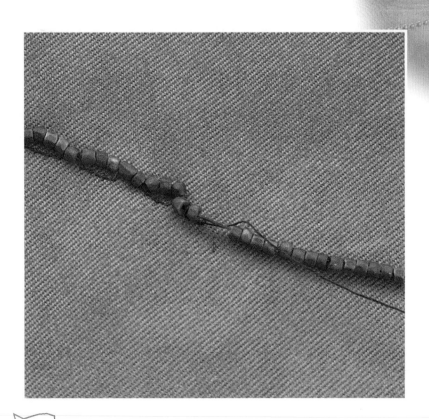

Alternate method. Set machine for blindhem stitch, so that straight stitches align to the right side of the strung beads and left-hand stitch jumps over string between two beads.

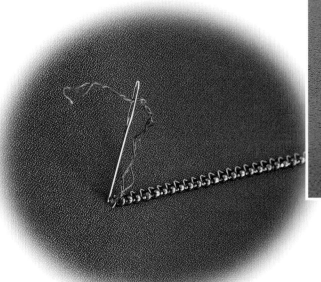

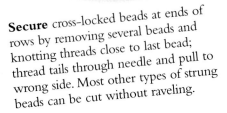

Secure cross-locked beads at ends of rows by removing several beads and knotting threads close to last bead; thread tails through needle and pull to wrong side. Most other types of strung beads can be cut without raveling.

String beads that are too large to fit under a beading foot onto beading bobbin (opposite); secure end to wrong side. Stitch in free motion along intended path; trail beads to one side ahead of needle. Move bead string from one side to the other every few stitches, stitching across string, to hold beads in place. Snug beads back before each crossing.

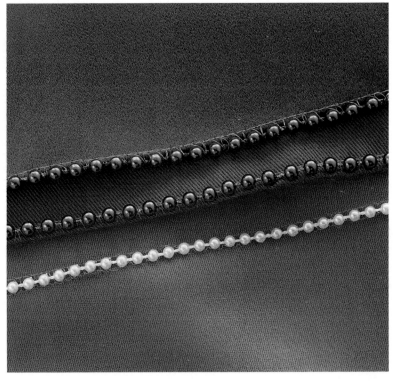

Attach beading foot to serger. Use monofilament nylon thread in right needle and loopers. Adjust stitch length to match bead size. Set machine for desired stitch: rolled hem (top) lays beads off edge, for reversible finish; 3-thread overlock (center) lays beads on finished fabric edge; flatlocking on a fold (bottom) couches beading in straight lines across the fabric surface.

1 Lower or cover feed dogs; remove presser foot. Set machine for straight stitch. Draw bobbin thread to right side of fabric at desired starting point. Stitch several tiny stitches; stop. Trim off thread tails.

2 Hold bead, hole up, one bead length away from thread exit point, using tweezers. Move fabric under needle until tip aligns to hole. Slowly guide needle down through bead hole; release bead and complete stitch.

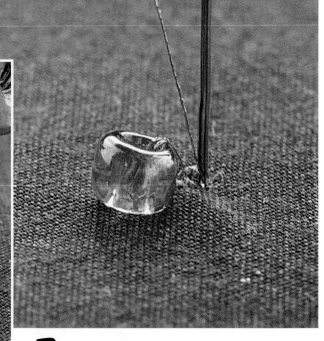

3 Insert needle into original thread exit point; complete stitch. Stitch to next desired bead location, if stitch trail is desirable or invisible. Or tie off threads and move to new position, starting again with step 1.

Stop stitch. Bring needle up through primary bead and seed bead on right side of fabric; seed bead is called the "stop." Bring needle back through primary bead, then down through fabric to wrong side. This stitch is frequently used for attaching single large beads, or a bugle bead that stands on end, or a roundel.

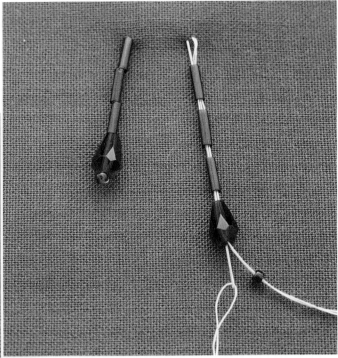

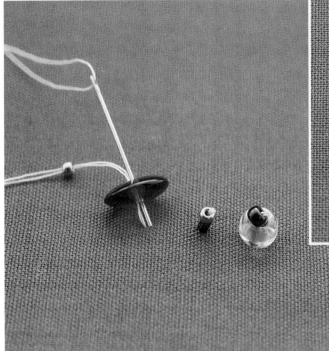

Dangle stitch. Bring needle up through several beads on right side of fabric; the last bead, or the stop, is usually a small seed bead. Bring needle back through all beads except the stop bead, then down through fabric to wrong side. Knot thread on wrong side after each dangle stitch. This stitch is frequently used to create fringe.

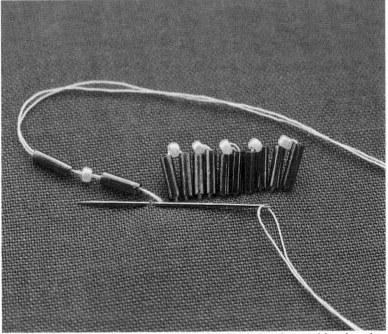

Fence stitch. Bring needle up through a bugle bead, a seed bead, and a second bugle bead. Take a short stitch so bugle beads stand on end. Repeat the stitch, creating the fence effect.

Edging stitch. Bring needle up through three seed beads. Take a short stitch so first and last beads rest next to each other; middle bead is suspended between them.

Backstitch. Bring needle up through three seed beads; slide beads down thread to fabric surface. Insert needle back through fabric at end of third bead; bring needle back up through fabric between first and second beads, running needle also through second and third beads. Add three beads to needle and repeat stitches. This is a secure stitch for sewing beads in a continuous line.

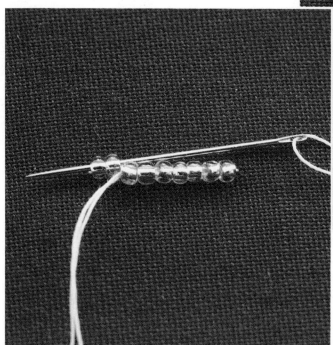

Filling stitch. Bring needle up through several beads, actual number determined by width of space to fill in. Slide beads down thread to fabric surface; insert needle back through fabric at end of last bead. Bring needle back up through fabric next to last bead; add several beads to needle and insert needle back through fabric next to first bead of previous row. Repeat, working closely spaced rows to fill in an area.

■ ■ Net-weaving ■ ■
on Fabric

Stitch a grid of beadwork on fabric to create an interesting border, fill in an isolated area, or accent the lines of a printed or woven check. To develop the rhythm of the stitch, it is easiest to work on an evenly spaced grid, either transferred to fabric or innate in the fabric's weave or print. The beaded lines of the grid float on the fabric surface, so it is recommended that, if the finished project will be handled or worn, the lines include no more than ten seed beads each. At each intersecting corner, a "point bead" is secured to the fabric, holding the entire grid in place.

Work the grid back and forth in zigzagging rows that run horizontally or vertically. Each row must have the same even number of point beads; the last point bead in each row becomes the first point bead in the next row. For additional accents, secure unique beads in some of the squares of the grid.

■ ■ ■ ■ ■ ■ ■ ■ ■ How to Net-weave on Fabric ■ ■ ■ ■ ■ ■ ■ ■ ■

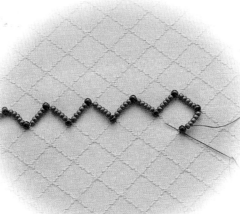

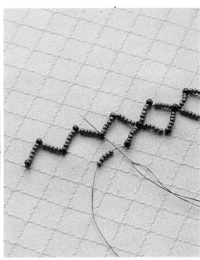

1 Secure thread at upper corner of grid; bring to right side. Secure single seed bead (first point bead). Thread desired number of seed beads, ending with second point bead. Lay beads along diagonal grid line; secure second point bead at second corner.

2 Thread same number of seed beads as in step 1; end with third point bead. Lay beads along next grid line in a zigzag pattern. Secure point bead. Repeat to end of grid row. Begin second row, angling back in opposite direction, and securing point bead at fourth corner of last square.

3 Thread same number of seed beads as between all other point beads. Lay beads on grid line, closing square. Secure to fabric, running needle through point bead and fabric. Continue second row, adding new point beads only to corners that do not join first row. Continue net-weaving until desired grid is complete.

Index

Creative Publishing international, Inc.
offers a variety of how-to books. For
information write:
  Creative Publishing international, Inc.
  Subscriber Books
  5900 Green Oak Drive
  Minnetonka, MN 55343

Sources

Decart, Inc.
(800) 232-3352 (product information)
DEKA paint products

Dharma Trading Company
P.O. Box 150916
San Raphael, CA 94915
(800) 542-5227
e-mail: catalog@dharmatrading.com
web site: www.dharmatrading.com
free mail-order catalog: dyes, paints, fabrics, supplies

Dick Blick
P.O. Box 1267
Galesburg, IL 61402
(800) 447-8192
e-mail: info@dickblick.com
web site: www.dickblick.com
general art supplies

Jones Tones
33865 United Avenue
Pueblo, CO 81001
(800) 397-9667
foiling products

PRO Chemical & Dye, Inc.
P.O. Box 14
Somerset, MA 02726
(800) 228-9393
web site: www.prochemical.com
free mail-order catalog: dyes & supplies

Rupert, Gibbon & Spider, Inc.
P.O. Box 425
Healdsburg, CA 95448
(800) 442-0455
e-mail: jacquard@sonic.net
web site: jacquardproducts.com
free mail-order catalog: dyes, paints, fabric, supplies

Sax Arts & Crafts
P.O. Box 51710
New Berlin, WI 53151
(800) 558-6696
general art supplies

Screen Trans Development Corp.
100 Grand Street
Moonachie, NJ 07074
(201) 933-7800
FAX: (201) 804-6371
foiling products

Silkpaint Corporation
18220 Waldron Drive
P.O. Box 18 INT
Waldron, MO 64092
(800) 563-0074
web site: www.silkpaint.com
silk paints, scarf blanks, patterns, kits

Sulky of America
3113 Broadpoint Drive
Harbor Heights, FL 33983
web site: www.sulky.com
e-mail: sulkyofamerica@mindspring.com
decorative threads, stabilizers

Testfabrics, Inc.
415 Delaware Avenue
P.O. Box 26
West Pittston, PA 18643
(717) 603-0432
PDF fabrics

Thai Silks
252 State Street
Los Altos, CA 94022
(800) 221-SILK
silk fabrics